arco*colour***collection**

W9-BON-108

houses

Private Mediterranean Houses

houses

Author

Francisco Asensio Cerver

Publishing Director

Paco Asensio

Proofreading

Tobias Willett

Graphic Design

Mireia Casanovas Soley, Quim Serra Catafau

© Copyright
Arco Editorial, S. A.

ISBN: 84-8185-015-2 (Complete collection)
        84-8185-017-9 (Private Mediterranean Houses)

*No part of this publication may be reproduced, stored in retrieval
system or transmitted in any form or by means, electronic, mechanical,
photocopying, recording or otherwise, without the prior written
permission of the owner of the copyright.*

Private Mediterranean Houses

Setting up house beside the sea implies a whole range of factors which make it possible to be located in the city while enjoying exceptional conditions of landscape and climate.

Open spaces, the long coastlines or the vast expanses of sea or ocean cause a reaction within the mind and body of man, whereas he reacts in a totally different manner to the faint light in the clearing of a forest or a valley encircled by mountains.

The architectural features of houses in regions with a hot, dry climate or a cold climate differ radically from coastal areas which are warmer and more humid. Even though each case must be considered separately and independently, according to the social and geographical features which may vary from place to place, there is a series of basic characteristics and general features which are clearly illustrated in the houses presented within this book.

For instance, these dwellings are distinguished by the lack of walls delimiting the property boundaries.

If they do have walls, they must be light structures which enable the wind to pass through freely. Shade, on the other hand, is an important element protecting the house against a build-up of heat. Eaves, covered terraces, porches and exterior galleries are some of the solutions which have been found for the problem of excess heat.

Another feature of this Mediterranean architecture is that the buildings are usually separated from each other, to allow the air to circulate between them. The large apertures (windows and doors) which cover most of the walls, constantly protected from the sun, allow crossed ventilation of internal space. The roof is also extremely important; this carries out the function of parasol and umbrella.

Beaches can be constantly lashed by the wind. Thus, roofs and decks must not stand directly in line with the trajectory of the prevailing winds. Canopies, air vents, blinds, shutters and outdoor furniture must be adequately protected against strong gusts of wind. The dwelling must be positioned in such a way that the areas containing most windows do not directly face the sun.

A closer analysis of all these features is of the essence, since they are the most representative features of the coastal constructions dealt with in this volume; this is borne out by the repetition of features from dwelling to dwelling and the obvious function of each feature.

This study of the architectural characteristics of Mediterranean areas where, in most cases, the climate is warm and humid, shows clearly that there is a series of features used all over the world for very specific habitats. Every one of the single-family dwellings described in this volume is a totally aesthetic example of the extent to which the environment affects human development, and how climate and the specific setting itself can determine the design and construction of the various dwellings planned by and for the individual.

Private Mediterranean Houses

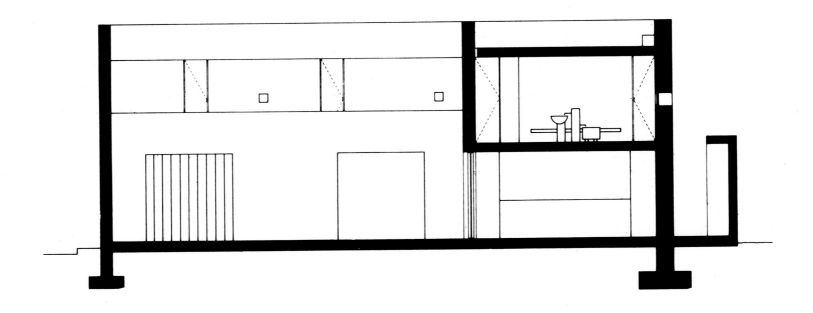

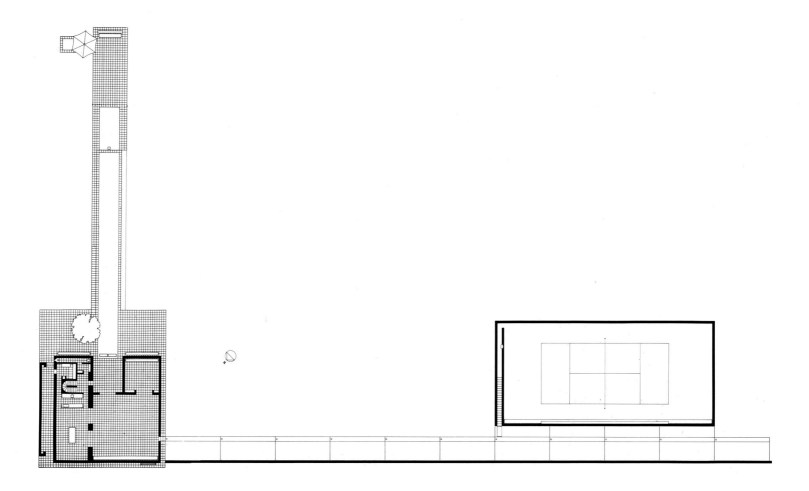

Section that shows two of the levels of the house.

Floor plan of the house.

Neuendorf Villa

Claudio Silvestrin

Born in Milan in 1954, Claudio Silvestrin studied art, philosophy and architecture, receiving his degree from the London Architectural Association in 1985. He founded the Pawson Silvestrin Partnership that same year. In 1987 he began to work independently and two years later he set up his own practice. Throughout his brief career, his fundamental aim has been to break with academic conventionalism (following in the footsteps of Barragán, Ando and Dom van der Laan). He gave various lectures at the London Art Fair (1989), Portsmouth Polytechnic, Oxford Polytechnic and Buckinghamshire College of Higher Education (1990). His projects and theoretical writings have been published in prominent architectural journals, and his most outstanding projects are the London Miro House, the Victoria Miro Gallery in Florence, the remodelling of a

Victorian building in Hampstead and, most important, the Neuendorf Villa in Mallorca.

Auxiliary facilities are often considered to be independent of the housing unit but, in the case of the Neuendorf Villa, they form an integral part of the architecture, establishing a relationship with the setting, rather than acting as a boundary. Underlying these central approaches is the influence of modern artists, such as Judd, Andre, Fontana, Charlton and Serra, as well as architects, such as Barragán, Gropius, Ando and Dom van der Laan, which transforms the architectural process into a philosophical and spiritual mediation. This project represents an exploration of the possibilities of family life within a formal, abstract, pure configuration, free from mundane, trivial concerns, and offers evidence that

Section of the different levels.

View of the pool from the interior.

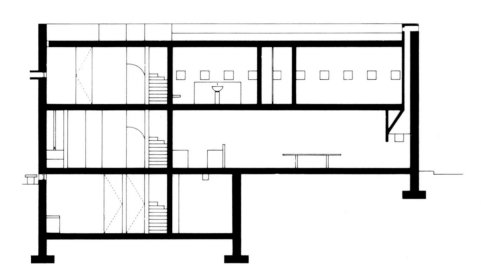

reduction does not necessarily imply nihilism and that a house is something more than a container for furniture. The systems of the perception and understanding of living space have changed with the fresh sensibility that defines an alternative to the present-day concern with consumption.

From the outset this project was conceived as representing a break with the conventional canons of the local Balearic architecture. Typologically, the structure does not conform to the customary building methods used in the area (the south of the island of Mallorca), the site chosen by the Frankfurt art dealer Hans Neuendorf and his family. However, the topography was a decisive factor in the development of the plan. If Silvestrin's proposal does not correspond formally to the indigenous tradition, it is

because he sought a more basic and essential communion with the setting. The Milanese architect's goal was a physical and visceral union with the essence of the landscape, which is parched and arid, marked by the reddish tones of the earth.

The total area of the site is 600 m^2 on which Silvestrin planned an imposing villa with a courtyard, swimming pool, tennis court and garden. It is a highly conventional programme transformed by the architect into a surprising and unique vision within the Mallorcan context. These factors are responsible for its singularity; the atypical relationship established between the architecture and nature, the exceptional treatment of the ancillary facilities, and the conceptual references attributed to the connection of space and form with domestic life. A more detailed examination of these factors will promote a deeper understanding of the mechanisms that governed the creation of the Neuendorf Villa.

Regarding the first of these aspects, Silvestrin's project is lent greater plasticity and expressiveness by the fascinating dialogue generated between the architectural configuration and the surrounding landscape. The house is executed in natural, local materials like Santyani stone, a sandstone that is similar to the Italian travertine. The outside walls and the courtyard were faced by means of a traditional pigmentation process, a mixture of sand, lime and earth. As a response to the dry red landscape, the walls are practically bare, except for the vertical slits that reflect the furrows of the earth and the interplay of light and shadow cast by the few surrounding trees. The relationship of the architecture with the countryside may be extended by considering the second factor, the outdoor facilities.

To understand the criteria used in the treatment of the facilities, the symbolic importance given to the act of entry must be appreciated. The villa is not directly accessible by car. Behind the country road that approaches the house is a shaded car park. From that area, a ramp/stairway, 110 m in length and built in local stone, leads to the villa. It has irregular steps and is flanked by a wall that gradually falls in height from 5 m to 1.40 m, dramatizing the entry process and offering an impressive and stirring view of the house. The route terminates at a 9 m -high opaque wall that forms the bare, blind frontal facade. The only interruption of this plain

The size of these windows is 45 cm.

View of the exterior.

The corridor is covered by a discontinuous structure that helps form an attractive game of light and shade.

View of the pool and the east facade.

The size of the lineal swimming pool 40 m x 3.5 m.

surface is a vertical slit, 83 cm wide, which offers access to the interior. The swimming pool is designed as an extension of the main volume. Forty metres in length and only 3.5 m wide, it is perpendicular to the access ramp. The pool marks the transition between the structure and the surroundings, serving as an imaginary liquid springboard to the earth. Between these two lines of connection with the setting, is the imposing, pure and rigorous volume of the house.

The appearance of the villa is in harmony with the landscape, but its composition does not conform to the typology of the island. The timeless and immutable aspect of the structure refers symbolically to ancient monasteries and medieval fortresses and creates the pervasive spiritual atmosphere. Through the integration of the static abstract form in the natural environment, the building paradoxically appears weightless. In this sense, it stands out against the horizon line, suggesting a Richard Serra sculpture that has transcended its dimensional limits.

In spite of the simplicity of the cubical tendency of the main mass, each of the four facades offers a specific, differentiated impression. The frontal facade with the vertical entry slit has already been described. The facade facing the swimming pool has a square opening, similar to a roofed terrace, that visually and physically links the interior with that long, narrow pool; its development is further extended on a lower level by the tennis court. Another of the elevations is a totally blind wall while the rear perspective is distinguished by 45-cm-squared windows.

Detail of the bathroom.

View of the main bedroom.

Detail of the stairway leading to the first floor.

The dining room.

This language, with its reduced repertoire of means and elements, is highly expressive and arouses tension and emotion in the observer.

After passing through the narrow entryway, the visitor arrives at a 12 x 12 m interior courtyard, around which is the L-shaped body of the residence. This space receives the same material and chromatic treatment as the exterior ramp/stairway. It has two internal facades finished with the same earthen mixture as the outside walls. A 70-cm-wide bench follows part of the perimeter of the courtyard. Simple quadrangular openings of a generous size provide access to the main rooms of the two-storey house. The ground floor is taken up by the collective living spaces (the kitchen, the dining room, the covered terrace that leads to the pool, and a study that has no physical relation to the rest of the

house). On the upper level the children's bedrooms and the guest rooms are articulated by a corridor that leads to the courtyard, which is roofed by an interrupted structure that generates a stimulating play of light and shadow.

The bedrooms have small windows, which act as shifting spotlights to diffuse a soft light. The forms and structural limits are drawn from the architect's minimalist language. The furnishings are subordinate to the overall grandeur and dignity. The simple, timeless travertine tables and benches designed by Silvestrin himself, the Hans Wagner chairs, the Barlow Tyrie hammocks of the swimming pool, the AG Fronzoni metal bed, the free-standing, cherry wood bathtub all contribute to the lyrical austerity and simplicity of a building that signals a return to the essence of a serene spiritual life in communion with nature.

N

Aerial view of the plan.

Refuge hidden on a cliff

Alberto Ponis

The rustic residence built by the architect Alberto Ponis is an ideal hideaway where one can enjoy the music and peace of the sea at any time of year. In order to eliminate any kind of break in or interference with the splendid landscape, the house is integrated into and totally subordinated to the rough topography of the area, wedged in among the rocks and vegetation.

This house is located in Sardinia, one of the larger islands of the western Mediterranean. The site, on the edge of a very steep cliff which drops down sharply to the sea, is strewn with huge granite rocks which have been broken and weathered into varied and curious plastic forms. Its privileged position means the inhabitants can enjoy beautiful views of the coastline and the islands of Maddalena and Caprera seen below the

house. On a clear day, the larger island of Corsica can also be seen on the distant horizon. The area around the site is covered with natural vegetation; typically Mediterranean bushes combining yellowish hues mixed with more intense greens.

Alberto Ponis was born in Genoa, Italy in 1933. He studied Architecture at the University of Florence, and in 1960 he began his career as a professional architect in London, England, where he worked with Ernö Goldfinger and Denys Lasdun. He went freelance in 1964, using his own studio in Palua, Sardinia, and another studio in Genoa. He worked with his wife Annarita, an engineer, and his brother Aldo, a town planner. His architectural work includes public buildings (schools, town squares, town planning design), and also private constructions

The house seems to be projected towards
the sea by the terrace around it.

(single-family dwellings, shopping centres, theatres, exhibition halls), decoration and remodelling work on several buildings. On the island of Sardinia, he has built many holiday homes, country houses, clubs, villas, and sports centres, always paying particular attention to the problems of integrating the construction into its surroundings. His designs and constructions have been published in specialist magazines and books such as: Architectural Design, The Architectural Review, Architectur & Wohnen, Casabella, Domus, Interni, Meridiani, AD, and Ville e Giardini.

A road to the northwest leads to the garage, located on the upper part of the site, some distance from the main building. A narrow mountain path, serpentine and almost invisible, winds down through a small wood of

strawberry trees to the house. A short flight of steps leads up to a series of patios laid out on the hillside. The small entrance courtyard, a shady corner enjoying a view of the sea, is protected by a pergola. The kitchen-dining room opens onto this courtyard as well as onto a second, very sunny terrace, half-hidden among the rocks where the natural grass surface has been retained.

The first of these patios frames the entrance to the building. The social rooms open off one side of the small hall: a large living room opening onto a spacious exterior terrace, and the kitchen-dining room. The other end of the house is a nighttime area housing the master bedroom, which opens onto a wooden-floored solarium; and on the north side, beside the strawberry tree arbour, a guest suite, which enjoys a certain independence since it has its own entrance. There is also a sort of grotto formed by a series of immense, rounded boulders, and a secret passage leading to a lookout point, commanding splendid views.

Whether seen from land or sea, this rustic house by Alberto Ponis, far from being intrusive, is in perfect harmony with its surroundings. The fact that all of the paths leading to the house have been designed to look like jungle paths adds to this special sensation of serenity, consummating the almost perfect fusion between the house and the hillside where it is concealed.

All of the outdoor areas around the house, including the grottos and the invisible path connecting the rocky nooks and brushwood clearings, constitute a second dwelling space; an alternative house. These private and reserved corners are used for diverse activities expanding the habitacle area of the dwelling and enriching the open-air living. All of these features greatly enrich the relationship between the occupants and their immediate surroundings since the exterior is as inhabited and frequented as the interior, eliminating any sort of abrupt barrier between the two areas.

The building appears to be leaning outwards to the sea, projected towards the marine horizon by the terraces and the lookout point. All of the rooms open onto this southern orientation, flooding the interior with light and colour. As a protective measure against the possible excesses of the climate, all of the windows and

Detail of the facade and overhanging roof supported by wooden beams that extend into the interior.

Perspective of the concrete stairway in the terrace and the shadows of the rustic wooden beams.

The projecting roof protects the porch from the intense summer sun.

doors are protected inside with curtains and outside by shutters. The house also has a cooler, shaded patio where the always pleasant sea breeze can be enjoyed in peace. An unusual pergola made of tree trunks arranged radially like an open fan shelters and defines this space, distinguishing it from other outdoor corners where the heat is more asphyxiating. Projecting roofs and covered terraces complete this protective system.

Interior of the dining room seen from the lower level of the living room.

View of the dining room from the kitchen. In the background, the large picture windows affording a view of the sea.

A detail of the shaded porch and its surroundings.

The master bedroom connects to a wooden sundeck.

Interior of the kitchen with smooth transparent walls and tiled floors.

The main rooms connect to the porch. The sundeck is shown with the sea in the distance.

The plain white interior is in harmony with the rustic simplicity of the house.

Living room-dining room separated by a couple of steps, with built-in furniture and wooden roof beams.

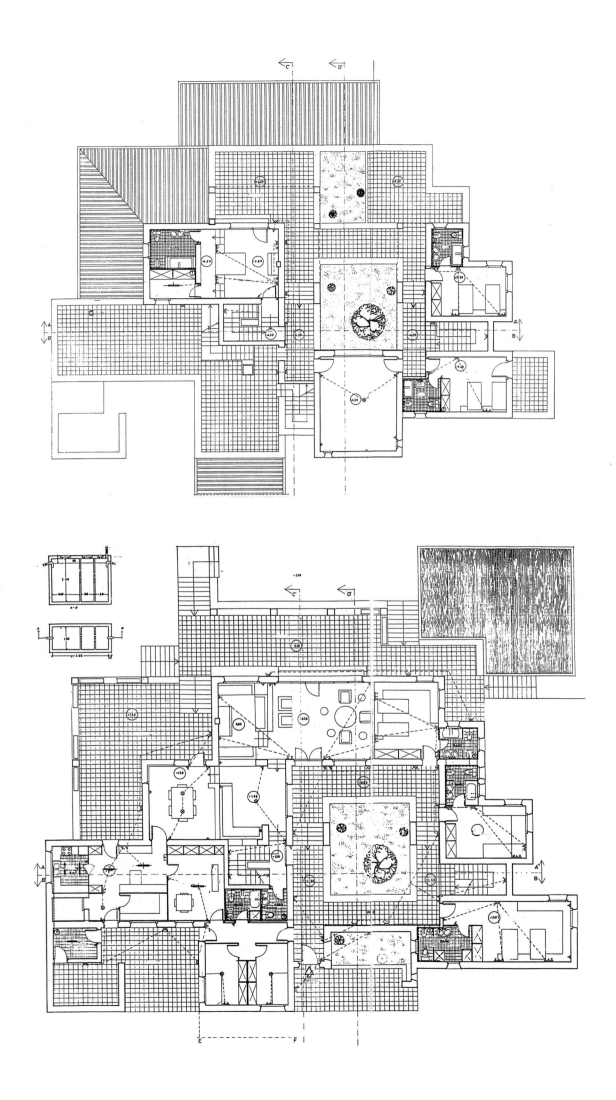

Top floor and ground floor.

Traditional Ibiza

Jaime Seguí Alea

Jaime Seguí Alea decided to build this house on Ibiza, surrounded by sea on all sides and nestling cosily within its warm sandy beaches. Furthermore this was no random decision, but rather a decision which points to the architect´s respect and fondness for the island´s architecture and the particularities of its unique culture.

Located in San José, Ibiza (Spain), this house is built quite high up on a hill which enjoys marvellous views of the island´s southwest corner and San Antonio bay. It is surrounded by a dense forest which acts as a kind of fence, separating the building from the sea far off on the horizon. The approximate surface area of this marvellous site is 30,000 m².

Jaime Seguí Alea was born in Palma de Mallorca, Balearic Islands (Spain) in 1927. He graduated in

architecture from Barcelona´s Escuela Técnica Superior de Arquitectura in 1959. He carried out additional studies in town planning at the Instituto de Estudios de la Administración Local, and qualified as a town planner in 1960 and as a doctor of architecture in 1962. He has lectured in technical drawing at the Escuela Técnica Superior de Arquitectura in Barcelona (1963), has sat on the governmental board for the Colegio Oficial de Arquitectos de Cataluña y Baleares (1972), on the board of Barcelona´s regional delegation of the Colegio Oficial de Arquitectos de Cataluña (1978-1979) – he also chaired this board from 1981 to 1982 – and since 1984 he has been a member of the executive committee. He has worked in a professional capacity since 1956, in the fields of architectural projects and site management – with

The buildings appears as a series of brilliant
white superimposed cubes.

commercial developments of office blocks, and also
apartment blocks or tourist centres, especially in Catalonia
and the Balearics. He has also won several prizes – he
was awared second place for his contribution to the
national prize for Rural Schools (1957), and won another
national prize from the Ministry of Education for a project
involving the construction of graduation schools.

This dwelling lies on a slightly irregular base on three
separate levels. The main block was constructed around
a central patio, with a hundred-year-old tree as its
centrepiece, around which various rooms, lounges and
terraces have been built.

An area of 153 m² of semibasement was allocated to a
garage, which can house eight vehicles and a workshop.
The ground floor contains three double bedrooms with

their respective bathrooms; the large internal patio
leading to the bedrooms; three lounges of differing size; a
winter dining room; a spacious kitchen with a cold room,
equipped with commercial catering facilities; a patio and
the laundry area; and two service rooms with shared
bathroom. The first floor has two rooms, one of which
has its own terrace and fireplace, and a workshop which
lets in a substantial amount of sunlight.

Large terrace areas and porches on various levels
surround the internal patio and indeed almost the entire
building. On one of these terraces there is a barbecue
area and an outside dining room. A large stretch of land
surrounds the building, including a 400 m³ swimming
pool, a tennis court and a large garden equipped with an
automatic watering system, all of which are artificially

The unit was built around a central patio, and around this patio the various rooms, lounges and the terrace were arranged.

illuminated. Access to the house is via an asphalt path leading to the entrance portico.

Jaime Seguí Alea's fondness for Ibiza, not far from his own place of birth, and its fabulous landscapes, stands out in the structure and attributes of his design. It was this very fondness which led him to build the dwelling in strict accordance with traditional Ibizan architecture and so incorporate it into its natural surroundings – the old white facings, the furniture built into the architecture itself, the staircases connecting both the inside and the outside of the building, the briliant white colour of the structure, the appearance of the structure itself as a series of superimposed cubes, are all typical features of the Ibizan tradition.

The sea is this Mediterranean island's most dominant natural feature, and thus the entire construction reaches

out towards it. On the one hand, Its privileged location on high terrain provides splendid views of the port and a substantial part of the whole island, which brings it closer to the mass of water. On the other hand, the system of terraces which extend towards the horizon and the swimming pool, the most striking feature of the facades of the building and which, in the distance, joins up with its blue waters, confirm this desire to merge. The dense foliage of the garden helps to unite the building and its natural surroundings, the nearby forest protects it like a natural wall, and the deep green of the pine trees contrasts with the brillant white of the walls and the coluorful flowers on the patio.

The connection between the outside and the inside of the dwelling is made primarily by the central open space

31

A large plot of land surrounds the structure, including a garden and a large rectangular swimming pool.

Views of the exterior stairway linking terraces and porches.

The stairs as interior and exterior connections are one of the features of the dwelling, most typical of the island's architectural tradition.

The dense garden foliage avoids discontinuity with the immediate surroundings of the dwelling.

inside the building, which enjoys the delights of the rest of the garden through its own symbolic content of the plants and the vegetation, and through sunlight, which is also a reminder of the garden outside. Secondly, the porches and terraces act as a parenthesis and reinforce communication between outside areas and enclosed areas. Finally, the large glass doors and the recesses in the wall facings constitute the third device used by the architect to make this connection.

The problem of excess of sunlight-exposed terrain was solved by a system of pergolas and shutters, protecting doors and windows, and also by the porches and open spaces inside the building which receved indirect sunlight.

The internal and external walls of the house are predominantly white. Likewise, the Artois tiling on the floors is used in all rooms, except in the bathroom where the flooring is of ceramic tiling from La Bisbal in the province of Girona. White plaster is the main feature of the walls and the furniture is mostly built-in, as in the case of the beds, which consist of raised surfaces acting as a continuation of the walls, covered with a simple mattress. All the bedrooms contain bulit-in wardrobes, and the woodwork is Oregon timber. The upholstery and the curtains are of soft shades and contrast with the colourful rustic bedspreads and carpets.

This luxury chalet by Jaime Seguí Alea constitutes an architectural banner, symbolic of Ibizan traditions and tastes, adapting perfectly to its surroundings and enhancing them with its extraordinary beauty and power. This sense of harmony thus becomes almost entirely complete.

The plaster on the walls contrasts with the surrounding green vegetation which protects the house as a kind of a "natural wall".

One of the porches contains an al fresco dining and barbecue area.

The problem of excess light was solved by a system of pergolas and shutters to protect doors and windows.

View of an exterior terrace at the top of a house, overlooking the landscape.

Plaster is a feature of all interior walls and the wood has been brought from Oregon.

The Artois tiling is repeated in almost every room except the bathrooms.

The porches and the dwelling's open-plan interior trap indirect light.

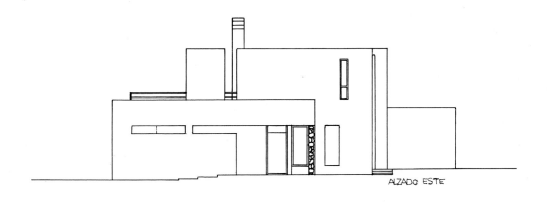

ALZADO ESTE

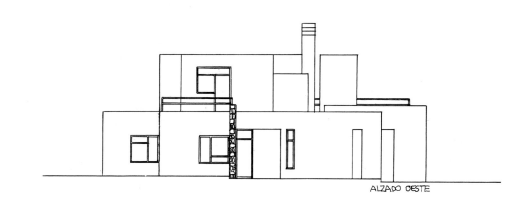

ALZADO OESTE

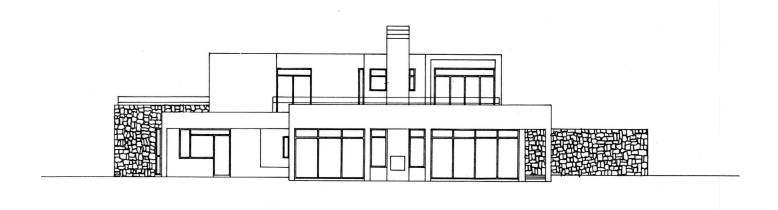

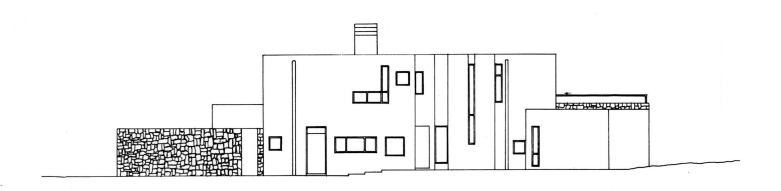

40

A general plan of all the different levels.

Vertebral wall

Luz Puerta and Beatriz Guijarro

This construction by Luz Puerta and Beatriz Guijarro is located on the island of Ibiza, where the white of the other constructions on the island, the ochre colour of the earth and the blue of the sea take on a special significance, helping to define and distinguish the structure.

The site on which the dwelling was built is in the Ibizan valley of Es Cubells, opposite the island of Formentera. The large site is on a slight slope, to which the house has a adapted perfectly. Surrounded by sea and mountain, it provides splendid views in all directions.

Luz Puerta López (Madrid 1961) studied architecture in the Escuela Técnica Superior de Arquitectura in Madrid, graduating in 1989 as a specialist in town planning. At present she is studying for a doctorate. She is also working on several projects with Salvador Pérez

Arroyo, a doctor of architecture, concerning the remodelling of Plaza de Cristo Rey and on various restructuring projects; with Enrique Álvarez-Sala, Carlos Rubio Carvajal and César Ruiz-Larrea on several projects for the Spanish Police Force; as well as with American Appraisal España SA, a company involved in real estate evaluation. She has also contributed to the book El paisaje y la carretera (Landscape and highway, 1986).

Beatriz Guijarro Regalado was born in Madrid in 1960. A graduate in architecture from the Escuela Técnica Superior de Arquitectura in Madrid (1989), she is at present completing her doctoral studies. Her work includes: 21 apartments in Noja (Santander, Spain) with the architect Alonso de la Joya (1987-1988), an office block in Los Angeles, California, restoration work on a

Drawing in perspective of the dwelling.

The ground floor contains most of the family areas. View of the facade and swimming pool by night.

New York apartment in the Otto Werner building, and furniture on this project with the Gwathmey & Siegel company in New York (1990).

This single-family dwelling was constructed during 1989 and 1990, and the two architects involved worked closely with Miguel Casariego Rozas, the site manager. It is a building arranged on two distinct levels on a large irregular base. The ground floor, which takes in most of the rooms and family life, is concentrated within this area: on one side we find three bedrooms with bathrooms; on the other we have the kitchen, living room and dining room. The last two are arranged around an interior patio and are the only rooms on this floor, which also includes an area slightly removed from the main zone, used by the night watchmen and connected to the main building by

the porch. The first level, which can be described as the most private area, includes a cosy lounge and the main bedroom which boasts the most privileged of locations, since it is surrounded by a system of terraces and exits, from where the occupants can enjoy the most splendid views. The large garden surrounding the house consists of a lawn and an enormous swimming pool.

When Luz Puerta and Beatriz Guijarro were considering the design of this construction they discovered that the sea, which the whole building overlooks, took on great importance due to the location of the site and that, in general, integration of the structure into the landscape and terrain would play a decisive role in the construction of the dwelling. The architects wanted the heart and soul of the dwelling to rise up from the very

Ground floor.

Drawing of the facade and the swimming pool.

The dwelling's walls have been painted white, the only choice given the climate of this area.

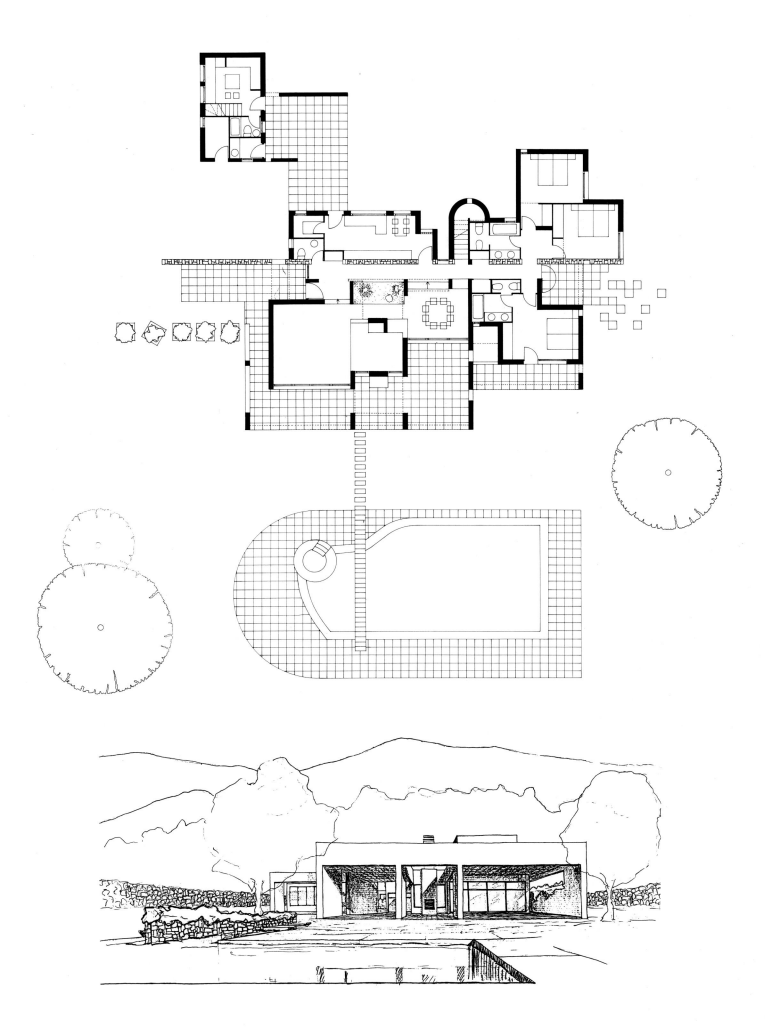

The house appears to consist of several white blocks which gradually take on their own identity.

earth, and for this reason they erected a wall of local sandstone – in this way local materials were shown some respect. Around this wall the entire house is arranged, comprising various white blocks which gradually take on their own separate-identities. There are two different situations on either side of the wall. On the one hand extremely open, intermingling spaces, in which wall and sea are the constant outstanding features, and on the other hand areas which deliberately shy away, linked to the outside only by small holes or recesses which provide a different taste of the valley in each case. Only one of these blocks manages to separate itself from the house, forming a separate cube with a double height interior – the night watchmen's club. In this way the dwelling alternates between open and closed areas, guaranteeing

freedom and communication with the surroundings, and also respect for the privacy and intimacy of the individual. The great variety of shapes of the bay windows allows much natural light to penetrate the building or, on the other hand, allows the light to be softened as it enters, in accordance with the function of each room, creating endless plays of chiaroscuro.

The wall provides access to the building and runs round it, finally arriving at small patio which blends in with the garden and which constitutes the intermediary connecting inside and outside. This function is also carried out by the porch, which wraps itself protectively around the dwelling.

The main bedroom shows evidence of a special independent character, since it is located in a privileged position on both sides of the wall. Here privacy is obtained by playing with the access route over the footbridge running parallel to the axis and facilitating a stroll around the building.

The facades of the large house have been painted white, the only possible choice given the climate of the location. Inside the building the plaster walls and ceilings are also white. On the lower level, the stone flooring is a light colour on the upper storey. In this way, as we go further into the house we grasp a definition of progressive privacy which is one of its main features. The drapes covering the large windows are likewise shrouded in clear chromatism. The furniture, tasteful throughout and not excessive in number, accentuates the filmy, limpid ambiance of the dwelling.

With this original design based on a vertebral wall, Luz Puerta and Beatriz Guijarro have succeeded in thrusting this construction towards the sea, transforming it into a refuge, and likewise an escape valve for the Mediterranean soul.

The entire construction is a system of terraces which open it up to the exterior. View of the swimming pool and the lawn.

A wall of local sandstone, since the two architects wanted the dwelling to rise up out of the ground itself.

Drawing in perspective of a room inside the house.

Drawing in perspective of one of the dwelling's exterior angles.

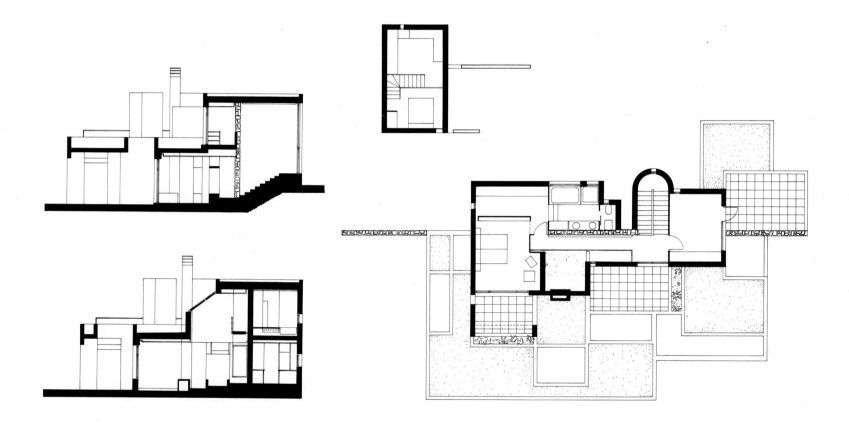

Sections of the house.

A corridor with stone supporting column
leads into the lounge.

Inside the house the white ceilings and
walls are plastered.

On the lower level the flooring is light-coloured stoneware tiling. Partial view of the living room.

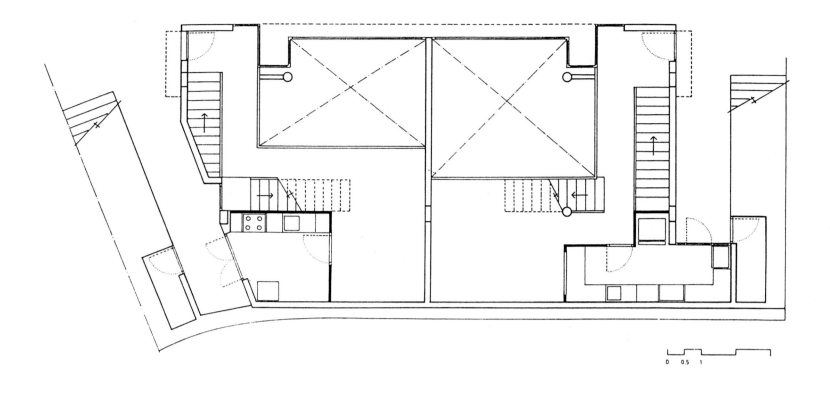

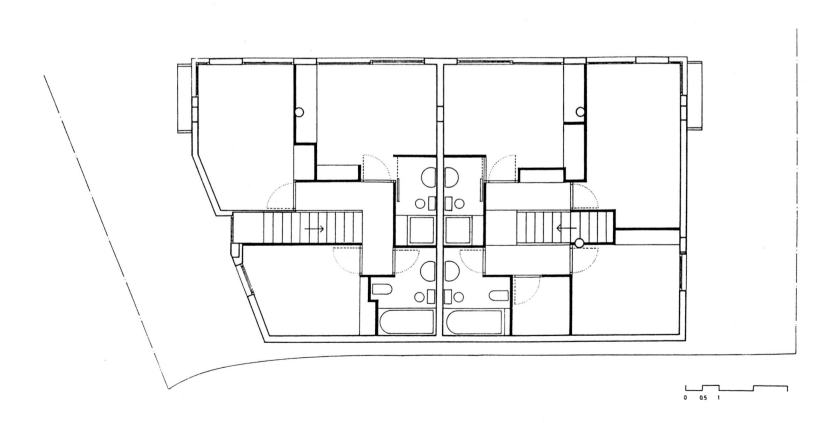

Plan of the first floor.

Plan of the lower level.

Nautical architecture

Jaime and Luis García-Ruiz

Matching single-family dwellings in Port d'Andraitx, Mallorca (Spain) by Jaime and Luis García-Ruiz.

In accordance with Luis and Jaime García-Ruiz's way of thinking, when two families decide to share the same house, to avoid any controversy the best solution is to design two matching structures which, despite being closely connected, guarantee the occupants complete independence.

The plot on which these two matching single-family dwellings were built was in the south section of the port of Andraitx, opposite a lighthouse, in the extreme west of the island of Mallorca, Spain. Between the access road and the sea the topography of the land has a marked unevenness; a natural phenomenon to which the constructions adapted perfectly. The site on which the

buildings were actually constructed has an irregular rocky surface and is surrounded by pine trees on all three sides.

Luís García-Ruiz (1946), studied architecture at the Escuela Técnica Superior de Arquitectura in Barcelona, graduating in 1970. He worked in the exhibition departmen of the Colegio Oficial de Arquitectos in the Balearic Islands, where he was in charge of the Miró 80 exhibition and, from 1980 until the present time, has been the municipal architect for Sóller Town Council (Mallorca).

Like his brother, Jaime García-Ruiz (1948) studied at the Escuela Técnica Superior de Arquitectura in Barcelona, graduating in 1972. Both architects work as a team. As far as their professional careers are concerned, they have jointly undertaken town planning and architectural projects. Several of their designs worth

Corner view of the house.

The house has many porches and terraces which provide views of the surrounding landscape.

Partial view of a stairway, and the surrounding landscape in the background.

The banisters and stairways have been painted white, as have the walls.

mentioning which have won competitions or prizes are: a building for a savings bank in association with José Ferragut, and a cultural centre in association with José García-Ruiz. Among their most significant architectural achievements are the remodelling project for the Palau Sollerich (1988), the renovation of patios in Palma (1989) and, in association with José Ferragut, the new head office for a savings bank on the GESA industrial estate (1990). They have also held exhibitions in the Palau Sollerich and in the Mallorca Exchange.

These symmetrical constructions were built on rectangular ground plans. The roof of the house, situated above sea level on the road, used as a parking area, provides access to the houses via two stairways at either end of the buildings. The dwellings were designed on three storeys. The bedrooms with bathrooms are on the top floor. The vestibule, kitchen and dining room are on the middle floor; both the dining room and the access area project over the split-level lounge situated on the ground floor, in such a way that the dining area is reflected in this desire for fusion and dialogue.

The covered balcony is in harmony with the surroundings; the white awnings covering it echo the sounds of wind and sea. The simple metal handrail, in the same colour, is reminiscent of the deck of a boat; in addition, it is the section which juts out most, appearing to lose contact with the land and sailing off into the Mediterranean, creating a strange and unreal sensation. The overall appearance of the dwelling, which stands out amid the intense green of the pine trees and reflects the

The four levels of the house are integrated in the
landscape.

All the exterior paving has been finished with the same white ceramic.

splendid light of this region, is white, clean and sharp, very much in line with the architectural traditions of the island.

There is a constant relationship between the different spaces of the interior. The split-level lounge connects with two of the floors; the dining room and vestibule are not closed off, on the contrary they loom over the lounge; and the bedrooms are openly connected to the terraces outside.

The way in which the architects used a variety of materials constantly reinforces the dialogue established within the property. Hence all the tiling, whether internal or on the roofs, is in the same white ceramic. The internal walls and upper sections of the external walls are all in the same shade of white. The handrails surrounding the

terraces and stairs have the same structure, format and colour. As a contrast, the lower sections of the walls have been faced in stone, so that they become confused with the rocky cliffs, reducing the enormous dimensions of the building.

Luis and Jaime García-Ruiz have designed a double dwelling which, in form, is reminiscent of naval architecture, evoking all things nautical. This allows the natural environment to be enjoyed to the full, an environment in which the sea is the indisputable main feature. The degree of dialogue and fusion established between the house and the surrounding landscape is complemented by the sense of unification and the spatial distribution inside, and is the underlying feature defining the structure.

Various stairways, lead down to the lower level via the exterior terrace.

Detail of stairway connecting the different levels.

The dining room is located on the intermediate floor in a double-height area in the living room.

Harmony between the surroundings and the dwelling's architecture is enhanced by the unifying nature of the interior spatial distribution.

Bright open spaces in a light-coloured interior.

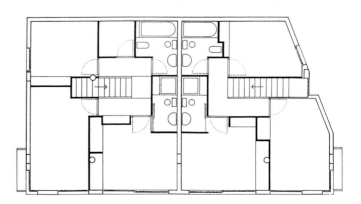

Floor plan of the house.

The interior is reminiscent of naval architecture. Harmony between the surroundings and the dwelling's architecture is enhanced by the unifying nature of the interior spatial distribution.

Detail of the metal staircase.

View of the living area from the first floor.

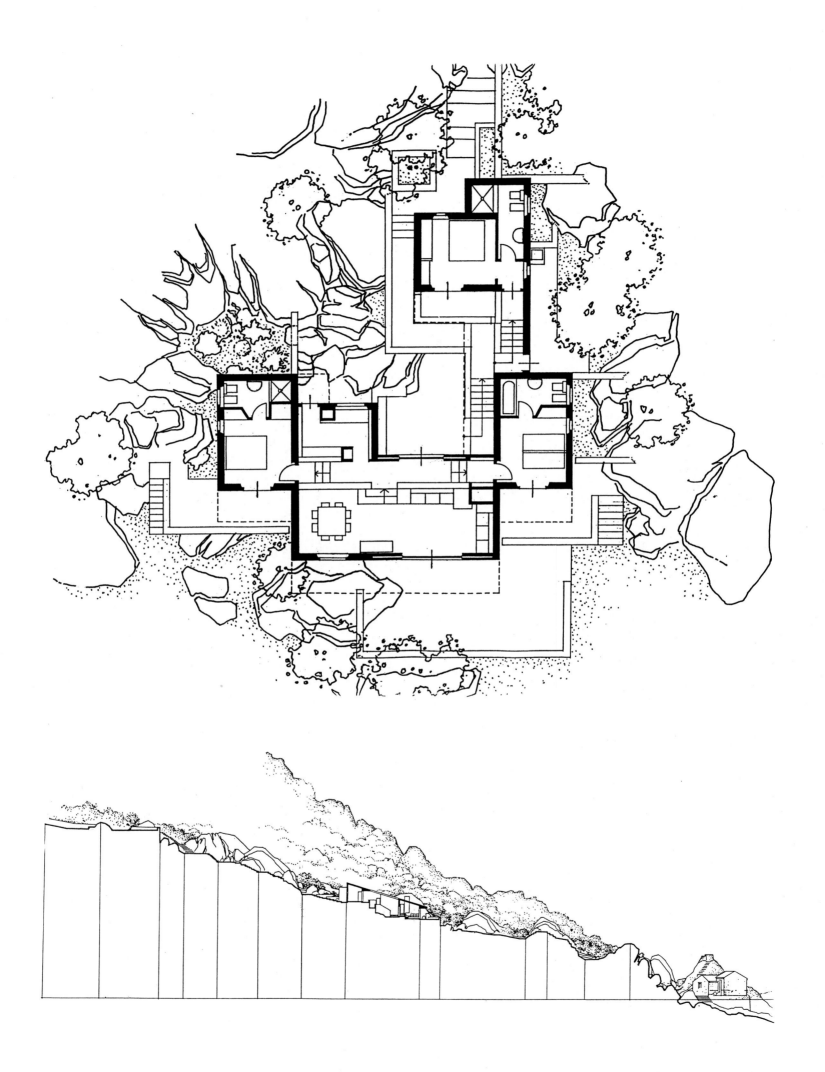

Plan of the house.

Perspectives of the house.

A house lost among the crags

Alberto Ponis

Alberto Ponis' love of Sardinia with all its rugged, uneven terrain led him to build a house which is literally lost among the rocks and crags of a spectacular cliff, allowing the topographical features of the terrain to dictate the structural criteria.

This single-family dwelling lies on the northern side of the Italian island of Sardinia on the Porto Rafael coast, looking out across the sea to the islands of La Maddalena and Caprera. The terrain has an extremely pronounced slope and much of it is covered by expressively and aesthetically shaped granite rocks. There is also a considerable amount of spontaneous vegetation in the shape of the scrubland so common around the Mediterranean. The construction adapts perfectly to this terrain, following the slope as it becomes more pronounced.

Alberto Ponis was born in Genoa in 1933. He studied architecture at the University of Florence and began his professional career as an architect in England in 1960, working with Ernö Goldfinger and Denys Ladun in London. In 1964 he began freelance work from his own studio in Palau, Sardinia, and another studio in Genoa. He worked with his brother Aldo, a town planner. His work includes constructions for the public sector (schools, town squares, urban planning) and also the private (single-family dwellings, shopping centres, theatres, exhibition halls, decoration and remodelling of various buildings). On the island of Sardinia he has built a considerable number of holiday homes, country houses, clubs, villas and sports centres, ever mindful of the problems involved in the insertion of the structure into its

Perspectives of the houses.

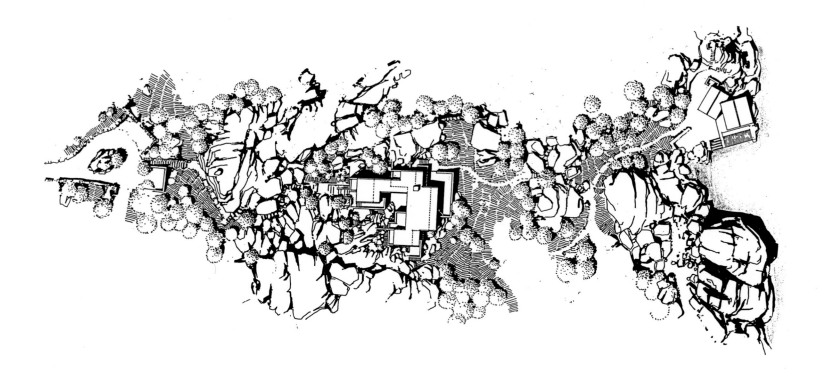

surroundings. His designs and constructions have been published in specialist magazines and books, e.g., Architectural Design, The Architectural Review, Architektur & Wohnen, Casabella, Domus, Interni, Meridiani, AD, Ville e Giardini.

The topographical features of the site called for an extremely articulated structure enjoying a very special relationship with the terrain, while also including mutual internal dialogue between the various sections. The various parts of the dwelling were arranged on several levels in the flat spaces between rocks and vegetation, closely following the slope of the terrain down to the sea. The final result is a sequence of rooms arranged around a central patio, open on one side and dominated by a large slanting rock. Access from the road and the parking areas

are located on a much higher level than the construction itself.

A narrow winding path leads down to the house and continues past it to a tiny bay, situated between a huge rock and an old military jetty. The latter contains two small structures built for use by the military, which now comprise an area used for afternoon siestas or a dining area overlooking the sea. Lower down via a stairway hidden among the rocks, there is an area called the "corner of the welcoming flowers", and beyond this a shady area under an enormous juniper tree. Both areas are outside the house, adjacent to the first bedroom with bathroom, which constitutes the guest room and provides some splendid views over the roof of the lounge, a separate entity whose only exterior connection is the central patio. On the north side of the dwelling, hidden among the olive trees, there is an area used for drying clothes. The stairs lead to the uncovered central patio, which includes an area for open-air breakfast. To the right of this area we find the kitchen and a bedroom with bathroom, the latter leading to the corner, ideal for soaking up the morning sun. To the left of the patio is the other bedroom, also with its own bathroom, which looks out on the Mediterranean and has a recreation area for the children. Steps lead from this section off into the rocks. On the seaward side the architect has built the lounge, which can be reached from both bedrooms, the dining room, and also the area containing the chimney and the day beds. Opposite there is a huge terrace which commands fantastic views of the sea, and a corner used for afternoon tea and siestas. This terrace is used for rest and relaxation. There are no corridors whatsoever inside the house.

The geometry of the dwelling's layout, in combination with the surrounding natural features, creates a series of well-protected intimate corners, similar to small natural patios which enlarge the building and add to the points of contact between man and the setting. Each intimate corner has a specific function or feature – the shady corner, the corner for drying clothes located in the most remote section of the structure, etc – which transforms it into an integral part of the whole. These external areas, together with the passages and steps which connect

The main volumes of the house are covered by a roof with a single slope following the slope of the land.

67

Two small remodelled military structures are used as rest nooks or as a dining room beside the sea.

The rooms of the house are laid out around the patio.

The walls are prefabricated concrete blocks plastered with a rough surface on the exterior and smooth on the interior.

The construction is totally adapted to the topographical features of the site, following the slope as it spreads out over the terrain.

Perspective of the tiled steps which connect the patio to the exterior.

The colour and texture of the materials make the house blend totally into the terrain.

them amid the rocks and scrub, make up a kind of the second house, which is used just as much as the building itself.

The relationship or connection between interior and exterior is therefore almost total; it is remarkable enough that the pivot of the design is the large slanting rock which was on the original site. From the building's open-air heart to the series of nooks surrounding each room, nature in all her vivid colours and pleasant sunlight is brought into the dwelling. Like the rocks set in the patios and terraces, the long passages and steps which the visitor finds between rock and crag constitute an additional feature which unites the house with its surroundings. The ivy creeps across the walls in an apparent attempt to take over not only the outside but

also the inside. It frames the large windows and the folding doors.

The walls are plastered prefabricated concrete, and the external surface is rough, whereas the interior surface is smooth. The colour used inside and outside the dwelling is light olive green, which serves as a continuation of the scrub and lichen on the rocks. This, and the unusual texture, help to fuse the house into its natural setting, a house concealed from intrudes who might disturb the privacy of the inhabitants. The main blocks of the building are covered with a single-pitch roof following the same slope as the terrain, whilst the kitchen and the three bathrooms have a flat roof of red tiles. Ceramic tiles, 25 x 25 cm, have been used to pave the exterior and floor the building's interior. The windows are protected by white

The furniture in the living room is built in, and the ivy creeping across the ceiling brings nature into the house.

View of the dining room with its smooth creamy-coloured walls.

shutters. There are several built-in bookcases, and the shelves are made of painted pith pine with brass metalwork.

This original building, which grants absolute priority to its breathtaking surroundings, rises up from its hideaway behind the expressive and whimsical shapes of the surrounding rocks lost among the green hues of the vegetation. This should come as no surprise to us, since the problem of the dwelling's successful integration into the landscape was one of the main preoccupations of the architect, Alberto Ponis, who has designed and built a refuge where the beauty of the Mediterranean and the warm shades of blue close-by are the only witnesses to a fine architectural creation.

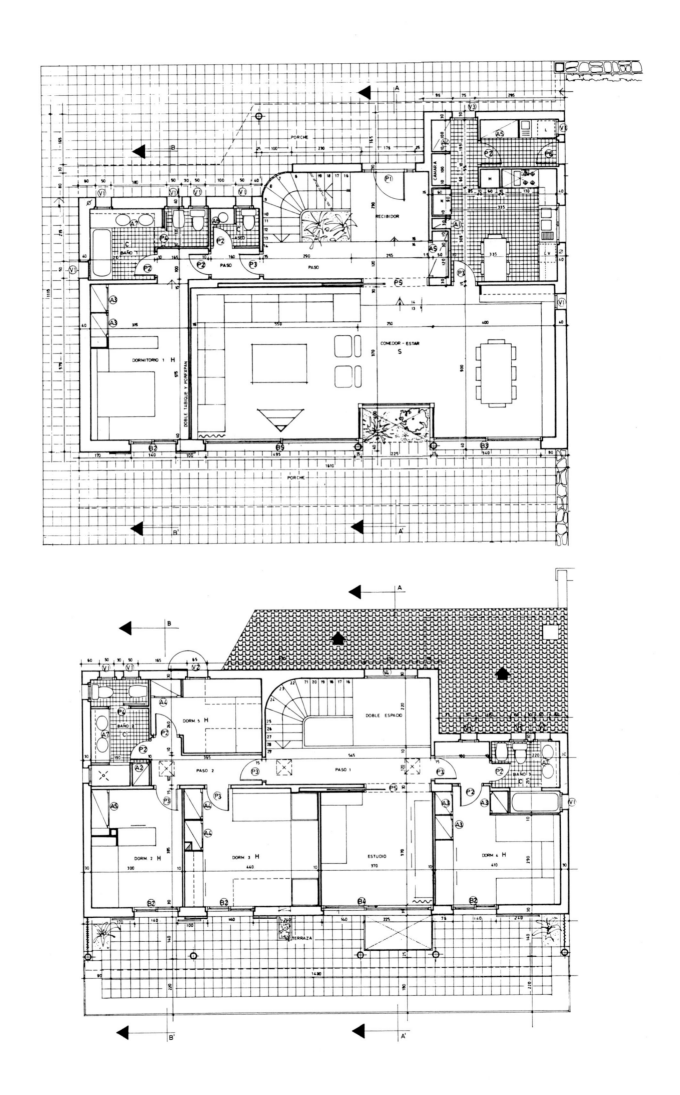

Pla of the tower level.

Plan of the main floor.

Mediterranean architecture

Germán Navarro i Borrás

This house is situated in one of the few green-belt areas on the left of the bay at Cadaqués, in the residential area Lo Castell which lies outside the town of Cadaqués.

The site is completely flat, surrounded by pine trees; the position of the building and its shapes were determined by the site itself, since the architect wanted all the main rooms to enjoy the amazing view of Cadaqués town and its bay, so the house was built at the back of the site. This created a large garden area at the front of the property overlooking the sea, protected from the scourge of the north wind. It also meant that maximum building space could be devoted to the facades of both storeys and to the terrace.

Germán Navarro i Borrás was born in Barcelona in 1945, and graduated with honours as an architect in 1970

from the Escuela Técnica de Arquitectura de Barcelona. He began his professional career as an architect in Barcelona, and also with the Cadaqués local council's technical department. He has worked in nearly every field of architecture, town planning and interior decorating, but his preference is the construction of the houses, for single family or several. The best examples of his work on single-family dwellings are to be found in Cadaqués, and this dwelling is one of his best. Navarro i Borrás also designed the Academy of Fine Arts, the Exhibition Hall and an office for La Caixa savings bank in the same town.

The ground floor exterior walls were constructed in Cadaqués slate, which acts as a socle for the upper level. This is a smaller unit built entirely of plastered brickwork, painted white to establish contrast with the blue of sea

Viewed from the bay, the luminosity of this totally white house stands out. The stone wall protects it from its surroundings.

View of the roof support column entrance. In the interior, the stairway through the glass wall.

sky and to create the luminous effect typical of Mediterranean constructions.

The main facade contains a structure which acts as a roof for the ground floor porch and as a floor for the upper level. Thin pillars which support the brick roof emerge from this white structure. The roof slopes slightly and features a white stylised chimney. This structure also separates the two levels and can be used as a terrace on the upper level, since it juts out from the structure as a whole.

The Cadaqués slate socle constitutes a base for the entire upper section, providing a colour contrast. The numerous glass windows allow sunlight into the building. At the bottom of the garden in front of the dwelling there is a stone wall which shields the structure from the

outside. The rear elevation has a small porch with a sloping tile roof, resting on a concrete pillar.

The building is laid out on three floors, interconnected via a central double-height lobby, the main distribution feature, which permits access to all the rooms and visual communication between all three levels. From this lobby the visitor goes down to the basement containing the garage, cellar and a perimetral extension of the wall which goes round the building and separates it from the surroundings.

This connecting room leads to the ground floor, passing through an exquisite hallway with antique furniture, and finally the visitor reaches the dwelling's centrepiece: a lounge/dining room floored with San Genís tufa, with white floor and ceiling and a Catalan, white

View of the facade facing the sea. Slender cylindrical pillars support the terrace roof.

Elevation of the entrance facade.

The facade including the main access is more closed and compact.

painted tongue-and-groove woodwork. Here the architect has sought to achieve balance between his combination of modern features, like the sofa or the built-in shelving with painted wooden shelves, and antique furniture – for example, the sideboard beside the dining room table which in turn matches the open artisan bickwork of the vaulted ceiling. This combination gives the lounge/dining room a particular air. The two rooms are clearly separated by a central area, and devoid of any decoration which might possibly draw a line of division.

The ground floor also contains the kitchen and the parents' bedroom, with en suite bathroom, connected to the garden by the covered porch which gently edges into the dwelling without, however, disturbing the architectural harmony, creating a small interior double-

height garden which also penetrates the first floor terrace.

Access to the first floor is also via the central hallway, up a beautiful white staircase with a wooden trim and an original curved white brick banister, leading to a corridor with a small square window in the ceiling which allows in sunlight and thereby floods the house with natural light. This window's best features are its simplicity and bareness – it carries out its function perfectly.

The architect designed a series of skylights which provides natural lighting for the entire first floor. This was achieved by the construction of a large study, decorated in the same style as the rest of the house and flanked on the right by the guests' bedroom with its bathroom, and on the left by the childrens' bedrooms and bathrooms, all decorated with wood and white paint. These contain

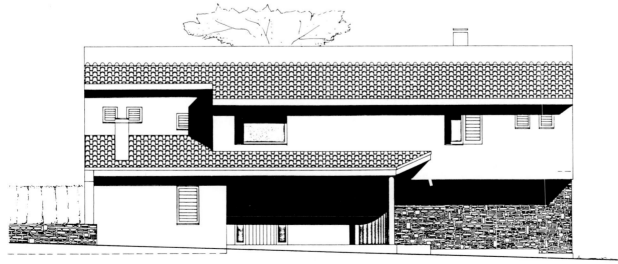

View of the staircase that conects with the upper floor.

View of the dining room floored with Sant Genís tufa, also showing an exposed brickwork vaulted ceiling.

windows overlooking the terrace, which provides a marvellous view of the garden and the sea.

In short, Casa Es Colom by Germán Navarro i Borrás is a harmonious architectural structure flooded with light, in which the placing of internal skylights throughout the dwelling and the construction of the terrace connected to almost every room make the structure shine out like a beacon, elevating it to a style of architecture which clutches at every feature of seascape and incorporates these features into the building, giving the structure its own Mediterranean character.

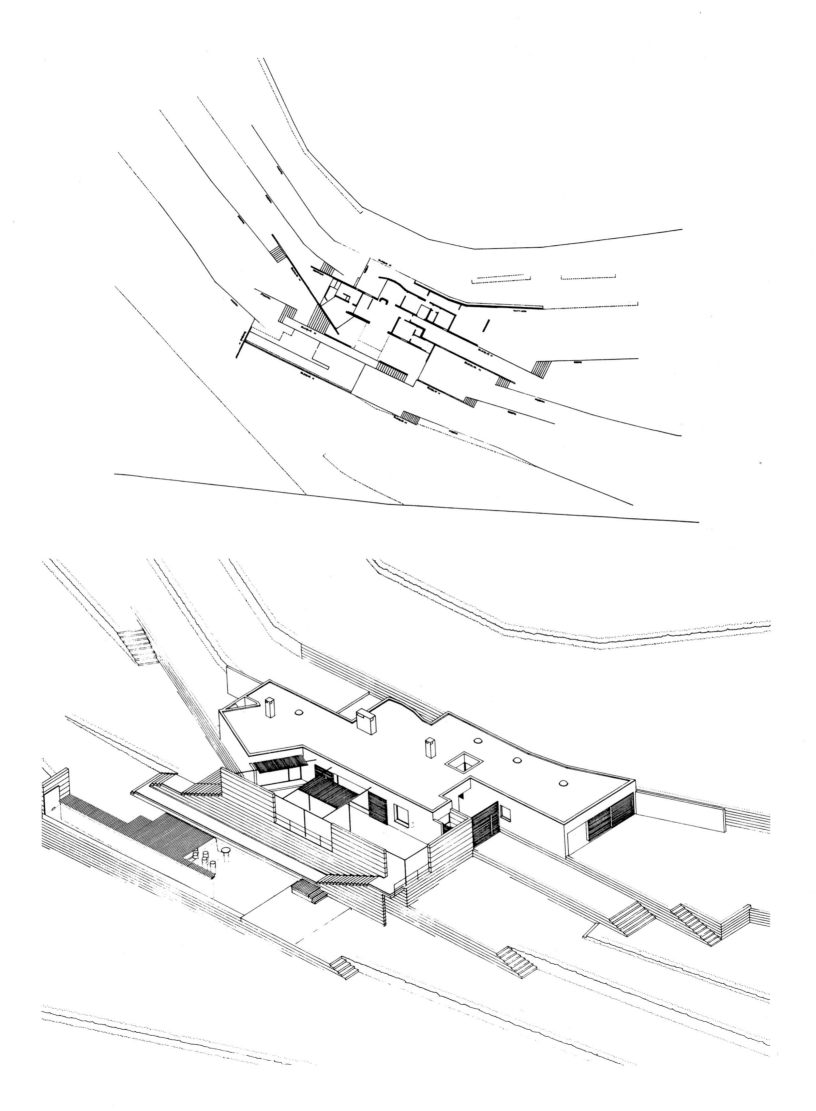

Axonometric perspective.

Plan of the main floor.

Spatial continuity

José Antonio Martínez Lapeña and Elías Torres Tur

José Antonio Martínez Lapeña and Elías Torres Tur, the architects who drew up the plans for this house, chose to create a single continuous space in which the dwelling and the garden could blend harmoniously, the interior with the exterior, work and rest with leisure and recreation.

This single-family dwelling was built on the island of Ibiza, in a luxuriant pine wood on a gently sloping south-facing hillside. The site provides splendid views of the sea and the bay of Sant Antoni, and the architectural components which constitue the residence have been perfectly adapted to the natural topography.

José Antonio Martínez Lapeña was born in Tarragona in 1941. After qualifying as a quantity surveyor in 1962, he continued his studies in the Escuela Técnica Superior de Arquitectura de Barcelona (ETSAB). In 1968 he graduated and set up in partnership with Elías Torres. He taught design, at the ETSAB between 1969 and 1971, and from 1978 the same subject in the Escuela Técnica Superior de Arquitectura del Vallés (ETSAV), in Barcelona.

Born in Ibiza in 1944, Elías Torres Tur studied at the Escuela Técnica Superior de Arquitectura in Barcelona where he graduated in 1968 and went into partnership with Martínez Lapeña. He worked as an architect in Ibiza from 1973 to 1977. He has taught design and composition (1968-1978), Landscape architecture and drawing (since 1979) in the ETSAB, and was visiting lecturer at the University of California, Los Angeles, in 1977, 1981 and 1984, and at Harvard University (USA) during the academic year 1987-1988.

View of the front, showing the swimming pool and the flight of the stairs leading to the house.

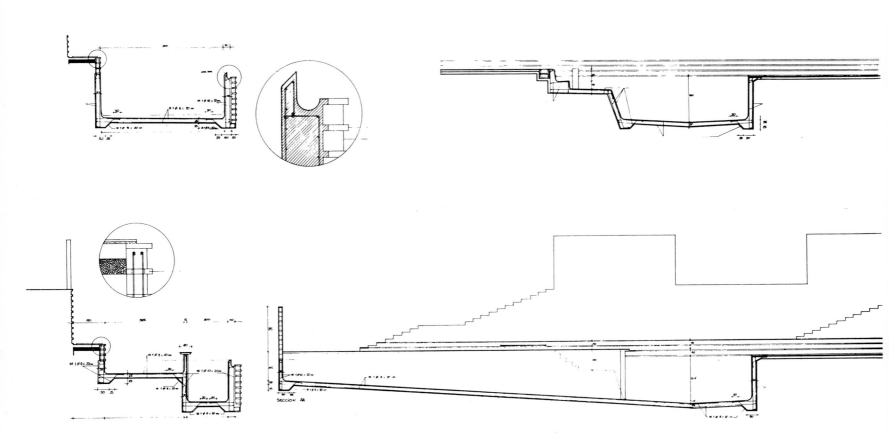

Different sections of parts of the house.

The space around the house is defined by a complex system of walls and pavement areas.

Section of part of the house.

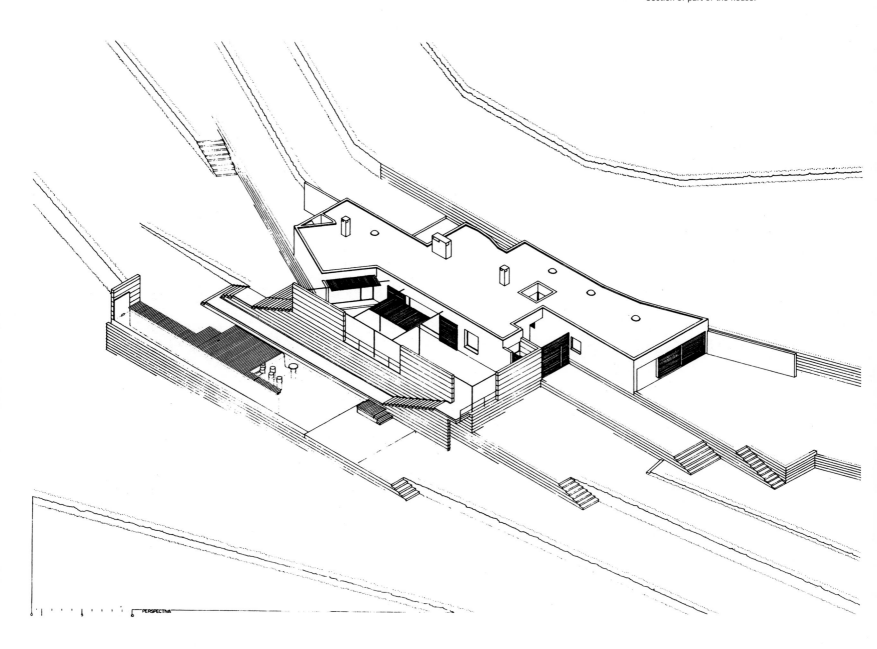

The architecture of this single-storey building is essentially rectilinear.

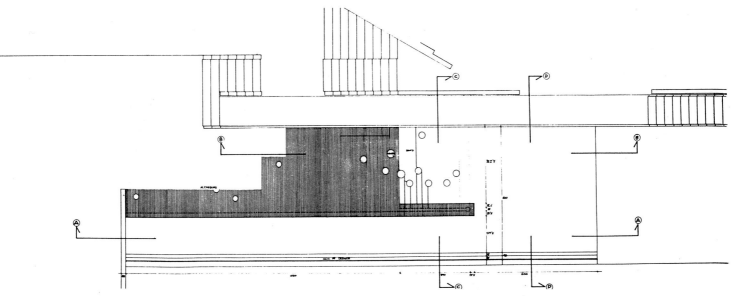

These two architects have won the following prizes for their professional work: Delta de Oro in the A*DI-FAD* for industrial design (1986) for the Lampelunas street lamp; the FAD architectural prize (Barcelona, 1986) for the gardens of the Villa Cecilia; Delta de Plata in the A*DI- FAD* for industrial design (1987) for the Pal-li canopy; as well as the FAD architectural prize (Barcelona, 1988) for the Hospital de Mora d'Ebre.

This one-level single-family residence is constructed on an irregular floor plan. The firm intention of the architects to avoid the creation of any kind of preestablished, artificial and unnecessary divisions, was the reason for this decision to construct a single-storey building. The house consists of the living and dining areas, a very functional kitchen and a study, which together make up the social area, and the main bedroom, or night area. All these different spaces are connected by a series of interior patios and nooks, which are open to the outside. The garden, which extends over a wide area, is equipped with a swimming pool, with a platform at one end, making an ideal solarium.

The architects' primary objective in this design was to create a homogeneous whole, unbroken by any interruptions of brusque changes of scene. For this reason, the external area has been shaped by a complex and intricate system of partitions, screens, paving stones, pergolas, and so on, which make it a living area, converting the different parts of the garden

The fragile materials used in the construction of the exterior architectural elements help to achieve spatial continuity.

The pool, square at one end, has a wooden platform at one side, ideal for use as a solarium.

The terrace, with a ceramic tiled floor looks out over the pool and the sea. The railing is white painted metal.

into extra "rooms", which complement the house itself.

The fragile materials used in the construction of the exterior architectural elements (for example, the wooden platform at one end of the swimming pool forming a solarium, the mosaic "carpets" used to pave the terrace, and the metal materials) reinforce this concept and very effectively break down the boundary which supposedly exists between the garden and the interior of the building, thereby achieving real continuity. In addition, a whole system of interior patios and small open courtyards has been created, which consummates this search for a connection and imparts a note of beauty. Even the walls, constructed with concrete blocks, which contain the earth and define the terraces, intensify the impression of a fusion between the buildings and the land.

One of the problems which the architects had to solve was the possibility of excess sunlight inside the house, a potential problem in the Mediterranean climate of Ibiza. In order to prevent this, all the windows and glass doors are protected with blinds and lattices which can be adjusted according to the intensity of the sun's rays, protecting the house from the heat entering through the interior patios and vertical openings.

In this design, Martínez Lapeña and Torres Tur wanted to ensure the constant presence of the sea within the architectural structure. In order to achieve this, a terrace was built overlooking the swimming pool and the Mediterranean. The effect seen from the terrace is a chromatic fusion of blues. The metal balustrade around the terrace, together with various marine motifs, such as

A corner of the interior decorated with local
ceramic pots from the island of Ibiza.

*the life belt and the navy blue canvas canopy, create the
impression of a ship's deck, and at the same time bring
the house closer to the sea on the horizon. In addition,
the porthole-shaped windows reinforce the maritime
appearance of this Ibizan residence.*

*From the outside, the construction is essentially
rectilinear, broken only by the pyramidal effect of the
flight of stone steps which encircles the house, and by
the cylindrical pillars which rise up out of the waters of
the swimming pool.*

*Both inside and outside, the principal colour is white,
which dominates all the components of the building.
Inside, the floors are covered with stoneware tiles and the
ceilings are crossed by wooden beams. The furniture has
been designed to provide ease and comfort. Light*

*colours have been used throughout the house for the
carpets, sofas and curtains.*

*In a dense thicket of intensely green vegetation,
Martínez Lapeña and Torres Tur have created a hidden
refuge protected from the outside world by walls and
lattice screens. They have achieved a powerful sense of
communication between the various parts of the house
and its marine surroundings, communication capable of
defying any kind of imposed barrier or division. The result
is that the house invites us, without hesitation, to rest and
meditate, in a peaceful setting only penetrated by the
gentle murmur of wind and the sea.*

The bedroom furniture is a simple and comfortable. All of the decorative elements are in pale colours.

The dining room is separate from the living room, connected only by a few steps.

White is the predominant colour used on all of the walls in the house.

Black-veined marble bathroom, where a lattice screen protects the window; the floor is tiled.

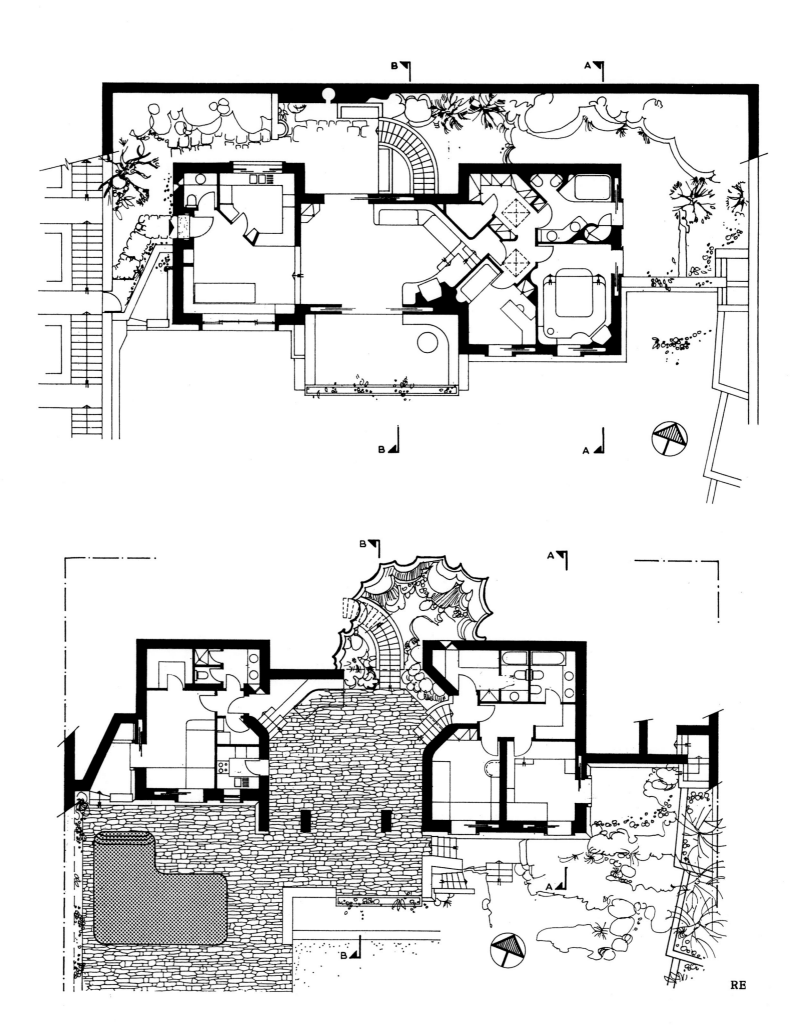

RE

Landscape extension

Michel Photiadis

This house, built in Porto Rafti bay on the outskirts of Athens, forms part of a group of rented dwellings. It was built quite high on a slight slope surrounding the bay, and thus towers over the sea on fairly steep terrain. The design nevertheless shows absolute respect for the surrounding landscape, and this can be seen in the colour of the building material employed. The house, in fact, constitutes an extension of the landscape since stone from this particular area has been used for the outer walls, and reinforced concrete for the columns.

Michel Photiadis was born in Athens and studied architecture in the United States. He has a considerable body of built work, including the American College of Greece, the Hotel Grande Bretagne, the Katranzos Sport department store chain in Athens, several tourism-related structures in various places in Greece, and a 500-room complex in the Résidence Gaston Thorn in Luxemburg. He has delivered lectures on architecture, and has also published articles on his work in magazines in Greece and abroad. He has won many prizes, one of which was awarded by the Greek Ministry of Housing for a group of traditional Greek houses on the islands of Patmos, Spetsai and Corfu.

This house was designed as a family holiday home. Its walls do not clash with the surroundings; on the contrary, they combine with the setting to form a coherent whole, since they have been executed with local stone. The roofs are flat and the columns are of reinforced concrete. At the front of the house there is a portico which forms the first floor terrace, supported by square pillars and

Making good use of the natural rocks: stone steps lead to a path made of the same material as the facade.

Sections of the building.

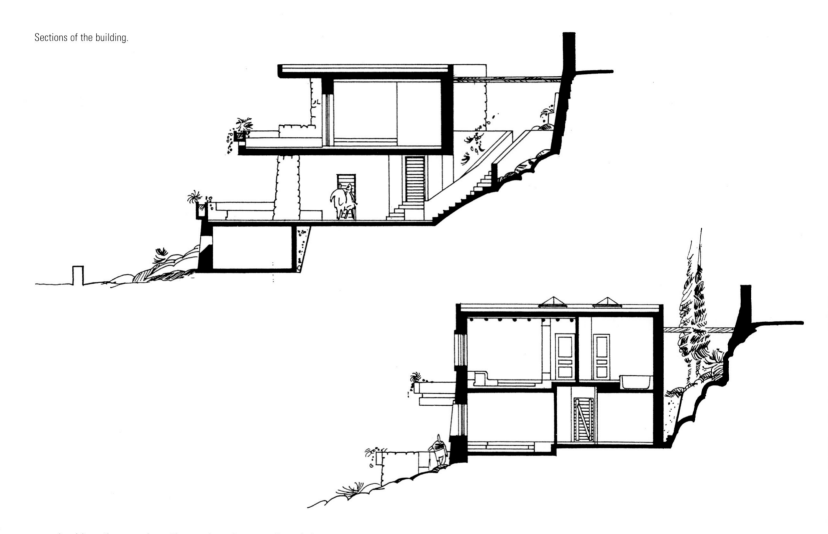

overlooking the garden, the swimming pool and the sea. The white portico projects out from the rest of the construction, and is decorated with red flowers which brighten up the exterior.

The spacious terrace leads to the garden with a view of the sea. It ends with a small stone wall which separates the terraces from the greenery which is the main feature of this part of the property. The paving stones are the same colour and material as the walls of the house.

To the left of the structure a series of steps lead down to an artificial path, also constructed with the same materials as the facade, which blend beautifully with the rocks and the original site, and could almost be considered an extension of the natural setting. The flowers and the plants growing here are also important.

They create an extraordinarily beautiful pathway and lend colour to the dwelling's exterior.

The main entrance is on the ground floor of the building, the chidren's area, containing their bedrooms and an indoor play area. The beds and the tables in the bedrooms have been built into the walls for practical and aesthetic reasons. On this floor there is also a small kitchen and a swimming pool. In this way, depending on circumstances, the house can be used as a whole or in sections, since each area contains all the necessary rooms.

A curved white wooden staircase links the two levels, from the children's play area on the ground floor to the patio between the lounge and the supporting wall.

The owners' private bedroom suite is on the first floor, which also contains a bathroom, dressing room and an

The roof of the porch stands out from the rest of the containing structure. It is painted white and decorated with brightly coloured flowers which give life to the whole exterior.

View of the stairs leading to a covered patio surrounded by the local rocks.

Detail of the barbecue located in one of the exterior porches.

This terrace connected to the living room opens onto a view of the bay.

This covered terrace is reached by a stairway coming up from the living room. The terrace is between the living room and the containing wall of the hill.

In the spacious living room, the built-in furniture is upholstered in pale colours, and the wooden crossbeams are visible.

office. The bed is situated in the centre of the room facing the sea, and thus even a person lying in bed can enjoy the marvellous view through two large windows, which also let in a substantial amount of sunlight. Its white plaster headboard is built on the brick floor, in contrast to the ceiling of superimposed wooden beams. In one corner of the bedroom there is a beautiful white hearth, also built into the wall, which matches the plaster of the bed. The bathroom is located besides a small private garden. The ceramic decoration was designed by Michel Photiadis himself and executed by Elpis Gianni. The shower is installed behind an extremely novel curved whitewashed wall and is a built-in structure, containing various shelves and a dressing table.

The visitor comes out of this suite and is faced with the wall, which is on the two levels; the upper level contains the entrance and an open kitchen with dining area. The tiles in the kitchen were made in Patmos from the architect's own design by Zorra Fetko, a lecturer at the University of Stockholm, and the ceiling is wooden beams, superimposed and separated. The lower level contains the lounge leading out to the two terraces: one on the left, towards the hillside patio, with a bamboo roof supported by an extension of the wooden beams inside the house, and a recess in the supporting wall; the other terrace to the right features a millwheel and overlooks Porto Rafti bay.

The spacious lounge has a wooden ceiling between the white sofas and the hearth by a small white wooden staircase which leads to the main bedroom. Two large frescos by the naïf painter Theophilus and an abstract painting by Stamos hang on the white walls. As in the main suite, the sofas are built into the walls and lend a most aesthetic touch to the room.

The dining room is completely separate from the lounge, and access to it is a via a set of steps. It has a wooden ceiling and a large window looking out onto a marvellous view. Michel Photiadis was responsible for the interior layout, which mostly consists of built-in furniture, the continuation of the structure of the walls in adherence to practical and aesthetic criteria. The walls are faced with smooth plaster, and the flooring consists of fired earth tiles made in Patmos from a design by Michel Photiadis. The same tiling is to be found on the dining room table and in the kitchen.

The architect was also responsible for the decoration of the house. He built the heavy main entrance doors of studded oak, and many of the splendid pieces of traditional furniture came from the Anthes antique shop in Athens.

This house built in Porto Rafti bay in nine months by Michel Photiadis thus constitutes an integral part of the surrounding landscape due to the local materials employed. The structure does not clash with the setting-it presents a smooth, functional, beautiful design, with some extremely original features in the decoration of an interior bathed in sunlight by the large windows.

View of the children's play area and perspective of the stairs leading to the upper level.

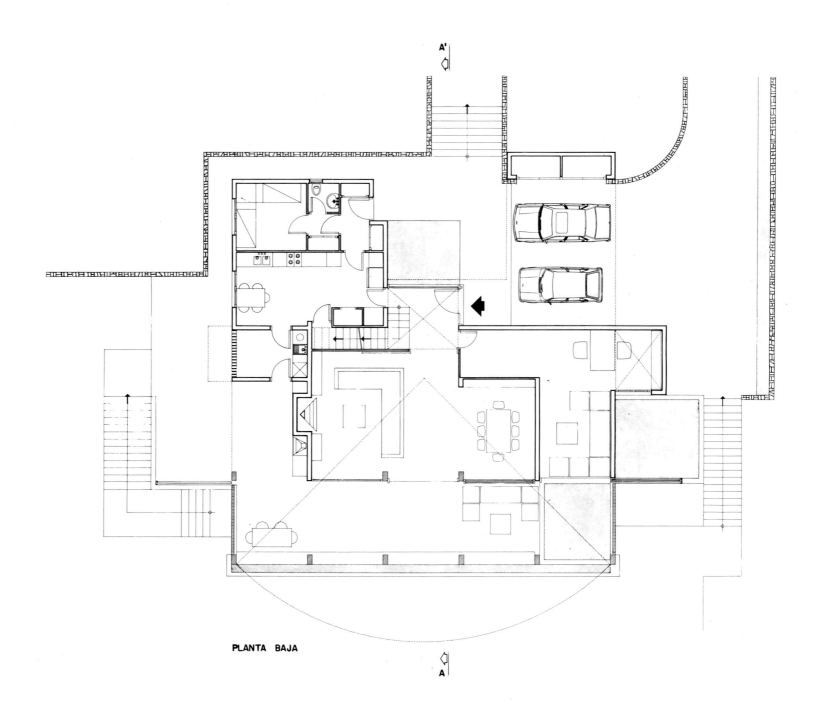

PLANTA BAJA

Architectural austerity

Pere Nicolau

Single-family dwelling in Mallorca, Spain by Pere Nicolau.

The signs of another language pour forth from this house, signs alert to the call of the sea, the pine trees, the slope of the mountain, a popular culture, signs inspired by the echoes of geometry and contemporary architecture – the signs from this house are an example of what the awareness and professional qualifications of a creative architect like Pere Nicolau can offer as an alternative to the systematic destruction of the island's coastline.

This single-family dwelling is located on the southwest coast of the Spanish Mediterranean island Mallorca; more exactly, in Marmassem cove at Port d'Andraitx, on top of a hill with a very pronounced slope and a thick pine forest as its surrounding features. It has been inserted into the landscape with all due respect, adapting to the slope of the terrain by means of its terracing.

Pere Nicolau (1948), studied at the Escuela Superior de Arquitectura de Barcelona, and graduated with honours in 1971. He immediately established himself as a freelance architect. In 1976 he successfully passed exams which gave him a place on the Ministry of Housing's official team of architects – in these exams he came second overall. He has been adviser to the Balearic Island's Town Planning Commission, technical director, a contributor to the Provincial Town Planning commission of the Autonomous Community of the Balearic Islands from 1976 to 1984, and since then has gone on to greater things. Among his best known constructions are the project for the next terminal building and access

105

This is an innovative construction since the blocks as such do not reject their basic expressiveness, and bask among the pine trees in celebration of their artistic excellence.

Outside the dwelling, any features which are not stone or glass have been painted white. View of the intermediate terrace amid the vegetation.

The composition of the dwelling's facades show hints of purism inspired by Le Corbusier – subtle simplicity of construction which has been carefully measured and well thought out.

The integral lighting system is a sculpture composition.

Curved and squared lines form the exterior structure of the house.

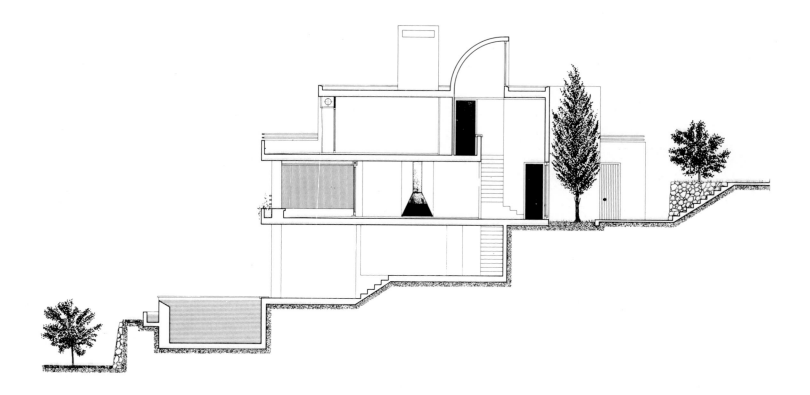

Section of the dwelling.

Terrace on the upper storey, commanding views of the landscape. This is the suntrap area.

The house is clearly meant to be facing the sea in order to capture light from the north.

At ground level beside the pool are the bathrooms for the children and sports activities. This is the sports and leisure area.

routes to Palma de Mallorca airport, in partnership with two other companies, INITEC and 3T; the remodelling of the Sagrera promenade which, along with the Parc del Mar (1984) and the Parc de Sa Feixina (1987), constitues the basis of the sea front construction of Palma's Old Town. He has won several prizes and his work has been published in specialist magazines such as Architecture d'Aujourd'hui (Paris), Ville Giardini, Interni and Architectural Digest.

Nicolau laid out the area for family life in this three-storey dwelling on a slightly irregular base, following a plan devised for a normal family residence, with strong overtones of things maritime and austerity with no hint of humbleness.

On the ground or access floor we find a room leading to the covered terrace facing the sea, which can be glimpsed through the tops of the pine trees, the impressive dining room-cum-lounge, the kitchen and a library; this floor also contains the garage and service area. On the top floor are the four bedrooms and three bathrooms, one of the latter being a section of the dressing rooms assigned to the main suite. These rooms all open onto terraces which, rising above the trees, overlook the sea; these are the sun traps. Lastly, on the floor below, beside the pool, are the bathrooms, the children's rooms and the sport and recreation area.

The architect was confronted with two differing slopes when he decided to incorporate this structure into the landscape since, if on one side the surrounding terrain is respected by the terracing which not only falls into line with the island's architectural tradition, but also *establishes a relationship between the white colour of the walls and the texture of the rocks going down towards the sea, on the other side it rises up as an innovative structure because the units themselves lose none of their rounded nature, standing out among the pine trees with all the pride of a successful artificial creation. In this sense, the construction is profoundly Mediterranean in style.*

The Mediterranean represents an idea, or at least it has done so since Matisse's sensual gaze with regard to painting or García Mercadal's Italian notes on architecture exercised their influence on an area which constituted an essentially historical region, and whose effects on the world of poetry were yet to emerge. It is also an invention, the imagination of the creative artists,

captivated by the aesthetic features of the region, which gave meaning to what had been, for the island dwellers, no more and no less than physical criteria conditioning their existence. From time immemorial these people had been building with no thought or worry as to exactly what they were building, and so – almost instinctively – had created architecture (there is no one single form of Mediterranean architecture; there are many), styles of architecture in direct competition with the landscape, but nonetheless retaining their own gracefulness when contrasted with the natural beauty surrounding them. It was in this manner that Pere Nicolau conceived his Mediterranean construction. For all that, this structure does not smack of historicalism or traditionalism. The

A collection of Guinovart paintings and a sculpture in the lounge, wich has been spatially arranged in accordance with the owners' needs.

The hearth corner, with wooden ceiling and light floor tiling.

arrangement of units is modern, in the most noble sense of the word; the composition of the facades evokes a purism inspired by Le Corbusier, with a simplicity which is at the same time measured, well thought out and subtle. There are also hints of J. L. Surt, the creator of skylights which tone down the blinding sunlight typical of this region and transform, reflect and diffuse it into warmth.

These references are not, however, not examples of mimicry, but rather experiences which have been assimilated. Their best points have been extracted and the result is absolute strigency. The architect has not allowed himself to be seduced by postmodern exuberance. There is nothing gratuitous or anecdotal about this dwelling; the various units have simply, or even austerely, been arranged according to needs which shun

Baroque alternatives. The furniture, as unassuming as these units, constructed along strict guidelines, does not give lie to the purely architectural qualities of the dwelling, nor does it conceal these qualities – it emulates them and integrates perfectly into the whole. One might even say that it integrates constructively into the unit as a whole.

On the other hand, the solution chosen as regards lighting, by means of skylights and shutters, not only fulfils this task by guiding diffused sunlight into the building, but also becomes a sculptural component outside the house. The dwelling faces the sea: the intention being to capture light from the north and to demonstrate nocturnal presence without, however, giving away too many details regarding this presence, and so the house closes in around itself on the far side, with only occasional

Upper level plan.

Lounge area, opening up to the sea through
the large windows.

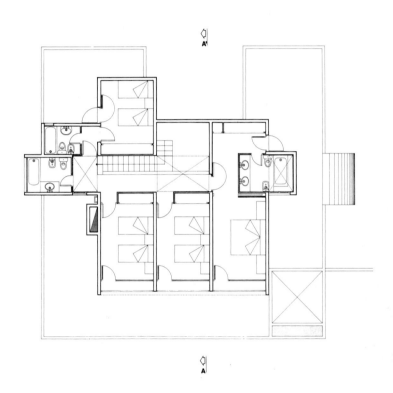

View of the wooden staircase connecting
the various levels.

Marble bathroom, with a detail of the mirror
reflecting the open window.

*openings, especially as regards the roofing; on the side
facing the sea, the glass and the white paint of the
structure give a sense of proportion to all the floors
– three units upstairs, five on the ground floor, and seven
in the swimming pool area.*

*Outside the building, anything which is not made of
glass or open brickwork is white. The walls, the pillars
and the hutters are of this colour, to contrast with the
blue of the sea, the green pine trees, the ochre of the
Mares quarry stone and the sky. All these colours and
finishes could be found anywhere in the world, but would
have extremely different echoes and responses, since the
spirit is necessarily bound to this sea, these pine trees
and this earth. Inside the dwelling, the white of the walls
combines with the soft colours of the stoneware tiling on*

*the floor, and with the wood of the ceiling and the
staircase connecting the two levels.*

*As regards the interior design of the house, the entrance
boasts an Enrique Broglia mural sculpture, of which there
are others in the garden and, similarly, a glorious collection
of paintings by Guinovart, several from the Banyalbufar
collection and also an original sculpture inside the house.*

*As a domestic landscape "domus" transformed into a
painting which frames the sea and the coast of Mallorca,
showing these from the terraces and rooms, this single-
family dwelling by Pere Nicolau presents an inviting whole.
The final result is a work of architecture which, without
rejecting any of its own subtle attributes, offers the
possibility of sortie, in the sure knowledge that, once
outside, it will be at one with the beauty of its surroundings.*

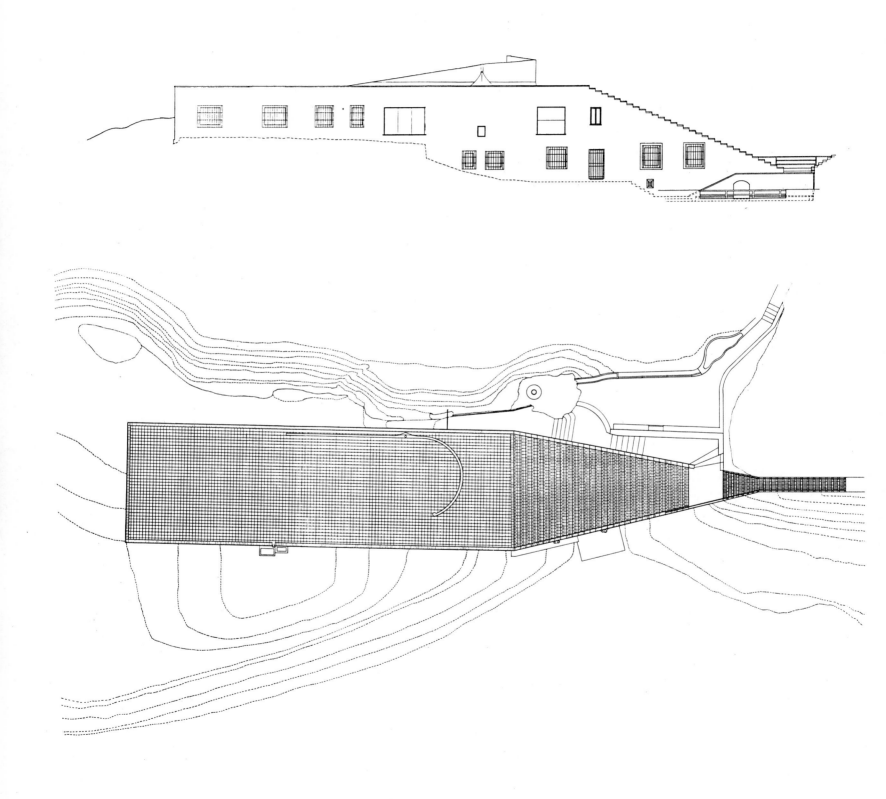

Architecture as spectacle

Adalberto Libera

The Italian island of Capri, an island of unexpected surrealism, is the location for Villa Malaparte, a dwelling perched on the rocky coastline of Cape Massullo. The blue of the sea and the sky, the green vegetation, the grey rocks and the brownish-red colour of the house itself make a contrast which lends even greater intensity to nature's colours. Nobody would expect to find an architectural construction on this steep cape running into the sea. It is difficult to imagine how it was possible to build in such a remote spot. The answer is that the owner of the house, the writer Curzio Malaparte, commissioned Adalberto Libera to construct this outstanding dwelling.

The writer, who was born in Prato in 1898, is the author of works such as La Pelle (Skin), was exiled for his political beliefs. In 1930 he visited Capri for the first time,

and later purchased several thousand square metres of thick woodland stretching from the rock called Matromania down to the sea, before he decided to have a house built for himself on it.

The person responsible was Adalberto Libera, an architect of international renown in the thirties, much given to larg-scale projects such as the Congress Palace in EUR, near Rome, and other buildings in the city, and for whom the Villa Malaparte was of secondary importance, since he and the owner did not see eye to eye on every aspect of the structure. The house as it stands today differs in almost every detail from Libera's original plan, since the writer himself became the author of this architectural structure – it was he, after all, who had thought up the idea for the location, unusual in itself.

The unusual setting means that the building
does not blend into the lanscape.

General plan of the dwelling.

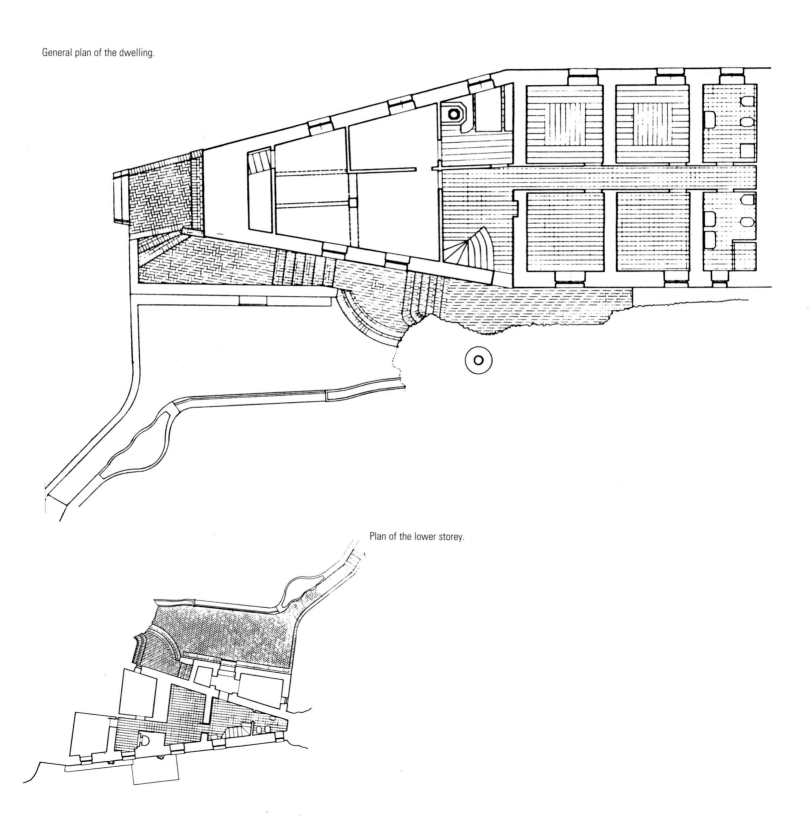

Plan of the lower storey.

The large terrace was made of bricks. The
white wall in the background.

The dwelling's large brick terrace commands a view of the surroundings.

Main living area.

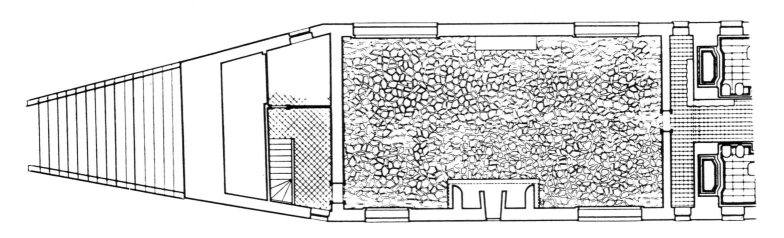

Room on the upper floor featuring wood.

The spacious living room is floored with
large, irregularly hewn flagstones.

Detail of the hearth covered with wood, and
a small window.

Villa Malaparte appears as an enormous wall, shaped
like a semipyramid of Pompeii red brickwork, built within
a natural environment. The main feature of the dwelling is
its inaccessibilit, and for this reason a footbridge had to
be constructed. It has a set of steps winding round the
rock down to the sea, which provide access to the house
but which are unusable in stormy weather.

The structure does not blend into the landscape, but
rather stands out and adds its own message to the
coastline of Capri.

Villa Malaparte is a long and narrow structure – 54 m
long by 10. wide. Thirty-three steps lead to a large
terrace which is the roof of the building, a roof so wide
that the writer used to ride his bicycle on it. This inspired
the cinema director Jean-Luc Godard to film scenes

there for his film Mépris starring Brigitte Bardot, a
landmark in the history of the film industry. It is built of
the same colour of bricks as the house, and endows the
house with that semipyramid trait which gives it such
character.

The house has two floors, cut off by the steps
leading up to the terrace. The visitor goes through the
glass door into the house and encounters a tiled hall
which sets the scene for the decor inside the house.
This leads to the kitchen and the guests´ and servants´
quarter; all these rooms are small and sparsely furnished.
Beside them we find a spacious dining room,
constructed entirely of wood with a flagstone floor. In a
corner of this room the visitor can admire a tiled stove.
This room has been given the name Camera della

Montagna or "Mountain Room" since the visitor looking through its marvellous bay window, can feel at one with the rugged coastline of Capri.

The carved wooden stairway to the floor above leads out of this hallway. At the top of the stairs the visitor finds the heart of the structure: an impressive lounge 16 m long by 8 m wide, tiled with large, white, irregularly laid flagstones. Unassuming wooden funiture decorates this room, with large swing windows providing the background. These windows look out onto the coastal landscape, in contrast to the view from the floor below. All the windows are framed in wood like gigantic watercolours. The room also contains a fireplace finished in wood, which also has a small window to allow the glow of the fire to blend with the sunlight and the reflection of the moon on the sea, creating an almost dreamlike effect.

A narrow corridor leads from this large room to the main bedrooms, placed symmetrically – one of which is called La Favorita, and is soberly decorated with hand-painted tiles in almost convent-like taste. The other bedroom belongs to the author, and it is decorated in the same style with a mixture of white colours, wood and tiled floors which are to be found all over the house.

The only indication of ostentatious decor is to be found in the two bathrooms, one for each of the bedrooms. They are of high-quality marble with built-in bathtubs in the art decó style.

Smooth white walls and sparse furniture in a sober living room in Villa Malaparte.

End of the staircase. The carved wooden banister and the ledge supported by spiral columns.

Partial view of the large room, its carved wooden door and the tiled corridor.

Simple wooden furniture against large swing windows.

From the owner's bedroom the visitor enters a large study, which occupies the whole front side of the house facing the sea; given this location at the "bow" of the house it resembles the bridge of a ship, a nautical comparison which is often the case in Villa Malaparte. It is T-shaped, with handpainted floor tiling designed by Savino painter, and has a background of the three windows offering a marvellous view of the sea.

In short, this building shows the conception of architecture as a spectacle, whose main goal is to make visual impact and to add a touch of character to a weatherbeaten landscape, achieving colourful play in contrast with the surroundings, within an interior overflowing with peculiarities and original touches; for instance, the daring stairway leading to the terrace. All these factors make it into an architectural structure in a style all of its own. Nowadays it is a foundation, La Fondazione Roncui, which sees to the villa's conservation, and it is occasionally hired out for cultural events or performances.

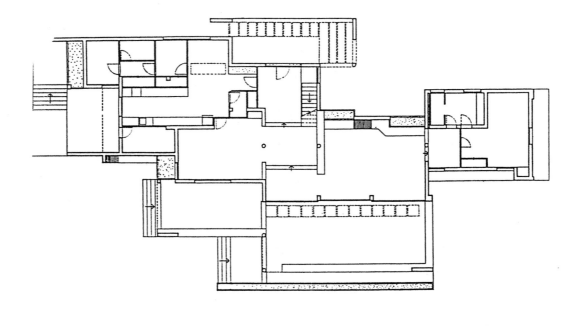

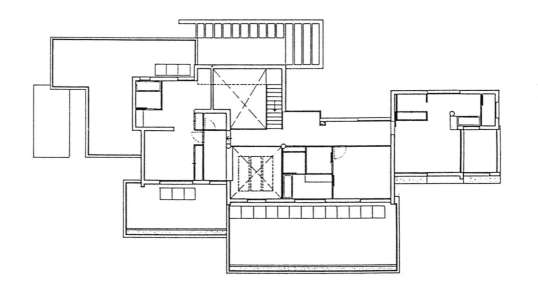

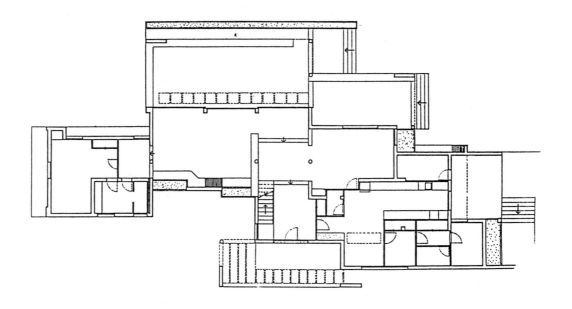

Glass surfaces overlooking the sea

Luis and Jaime García-Ruiz

In view of the location for this construction and its natural surroundings, Luis and Jaime García-Ruiz decided to build a single-family dwelling on a totally open plan which would project out towards the sea and provide some enviable views of this area of the Mediterranean and its rugged, harsh coastline.

This building is located at Port d'Andraitx, on the Mediterranean island of Mallorca (Spain), and has been built on a small hill which provides some extremely impressive views of the coast and the sea. A large number of pine trees grow on the site, surrounding the house on all sides. The site slopes sharply down to the sea. The dwelling has been built facing north to take advantage of the splendid views, and also because in this way it adapts with greater ease to the harsh irregular terrain.

Luis García-Ruiz was born in 1946. He studied architecture at the Escuela Técnica Superior de Arquitectura in Barcelona, and obtained his degree in 1970. At present he works in the exhibition department of the Balearic Islands' Colegio Oficial de Arquitectos. He is in charge of the Miró 80 exhibition, and since 1980 has been a municipal architect for Sóller Town Council on the island of Mallorca.

Jaime García-Ruiz was born in 1948. He also studied at the Escuela Superior de Arquitectura in Barcelona and graduated in 1972.

The brothers work as a team. Their work, which they prefer to carry out in Mallorca, includes both town planning and architecture. Their award-winning constructions include a building commissioned by the Caja de Ahorros savings bank, in association with José

Section of the house.

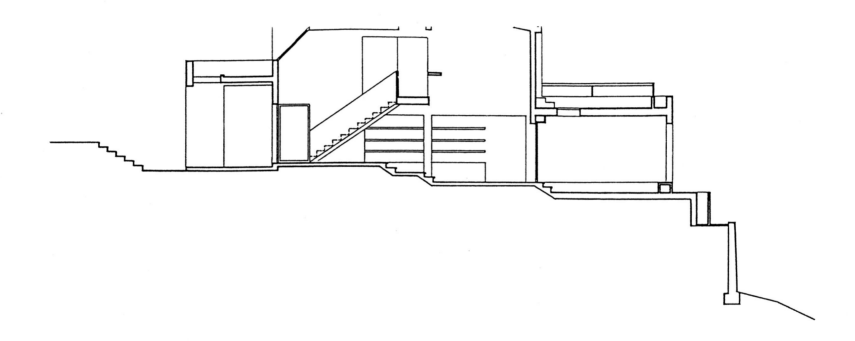

Ferragut, and restoration work on a large community cultural centre, the Sa Nostra, working alongside José García-Ruiz. Mention must be made of their remodelling work on the Palau Sollerich (1988), reconstruction work on patios in Palma (1989), and their design for a new headquarters for the Caja de Ahorros savings bank in the GESA industrial complex, working with José Ferragut (1990). They also hold exhibitions in the Palau Sollerich and the Mallorca Exchange.

Access to this house, built on an irregular ground plan, is across a narrow asphalt road. The structure consists of a series of cubes, with rectangular or square bases, set back. The two levels of the house are divided into a nighttime sleeping area and a living area for family and friends, thus following the classic guidelines of spatial arrangement.

The ground or access floor comprises a sequence of rooms including the main living room on two levels with various summer and winter areas, the study-cum-library, hall and dining room. These last two rooms are connected by a system of openings in the walls, and the only feature separating them is the difference in the floor level. The kitchen and its service areas are also located on this level. On the floor above we find the bedrooms. This floor is divided into two parts: an area for the children with rooms for work, study and play, and the parents' area which includes a bedroom suite with fully equipped bathroom and dressing room.

The access route to this single-family dwelling built by Luis and Jaime García-Ruiz faces south, whereas views of the surrounding landscape lie to the north. This arrangement constitutes one of the principal conditioning factors taken in consideration in the design of the building. For this reason a series of very private areas in the form of small gardens have been placed facing south. Their function is to seek out sunlight and direct it into the house. Meanwhile, on the north side, the dwelling's large windows bring in much light and provide fabulous views of the contrast between the deep green of the pine and the clear blue of the sea. Through the glass, communication is established between the impressive beauty and splendour of the landscape and the synthetic nature of the architectural structure. The porches play an implicit role in complementing this effect – they simultaneously constitute semi-open areas and

hideaways all but closed to strangers. However, to protect the building from excess sunlight and heat, so typical of the island's pleasant warm climate, all the doors and windows were fitted with a system of blinds and shutters which seal off the interior and also guarantee the privacy of the occupants, whilst the porches in the same area bring in softer, filtered sunlight.

The sea is visible from every room in the house, and constitutes the dwelling's most essential feature. The building itself, by means of the extensive glass surfaces on both facades and the strategically placed openings, is transformed into a permeable membrane which presents no real obstacle. The various structural features take on great relevance in this design. There is, moreover, almost

Most of the surface is painted white, although the construction materials are exposed in some places.

Stone stairway leading up from the sea to the house, where large porches filter the intense sunlight.

The structure consists of a series of cubes with rectangular or square bases, set back to back.

The house was located in the middle of a forest.

The structure is built on bearing walls and concrete pillars.

To protect the building from excess sun and heat, blinds and latticework screens have been fitted to all doors and windows.

total communication between the various levels, a sensation mainly created by the double eight lounge which also forms part of the upper floor; the balcony area above the staircase constitutes an unifying element, since it merely consists of a lath stretching from one side to the other. The rest of the balcony is left open above the void in defiance of the dizzy heights, and has an unusual volatile effect.

The basic structure of the house consists of load-bearing walls and concrete pillars; outside, most of the building has been painted white, but some parts maintain their original colour and texture, and blend in with the greyish rocky cliff terrain running down to the sea.

Inside the building the lower level has ceramic flooring, whilst the ceiling and the walls are white painted plaster. The classical rustic furniture combines wood with the soft colours of the upholstery, in contrast to the vivid colouring of the carpets covering most of the floor.

Seen from the access road to the north, this single-family dwelling by Luis and Jaime García-Ruiz demonstrates the intimate nature which makes it a perfect refuge, hidden away within the most beautiful of surroundings. Inside the building the visitor nevertheless discovers a totally different world, infinitely rich landscape towards which the construction thrusts itself, occasionally laying down its own conditions and shutting itself off when necessary, refusing to accept complete domination by another ambience.

The floor of the lower storey is covered with ceramic tiles.

Detail of the dining room area on one of the porches.

As on the roof the interior walls are plastered, with some white-painted areas and others of exposed material. Views of the double-height reception area.

Detail of a built-in plaster bookshelf in the living room.

The balcony-like stairway as a unifying element, appearing as a slab crossing the house from one side to the other.

Bath and dressing room of the master suite on the upper floor.

The porches serve to relate the house to the exterior; they are semi-opened spaces or semi-closed nooks.

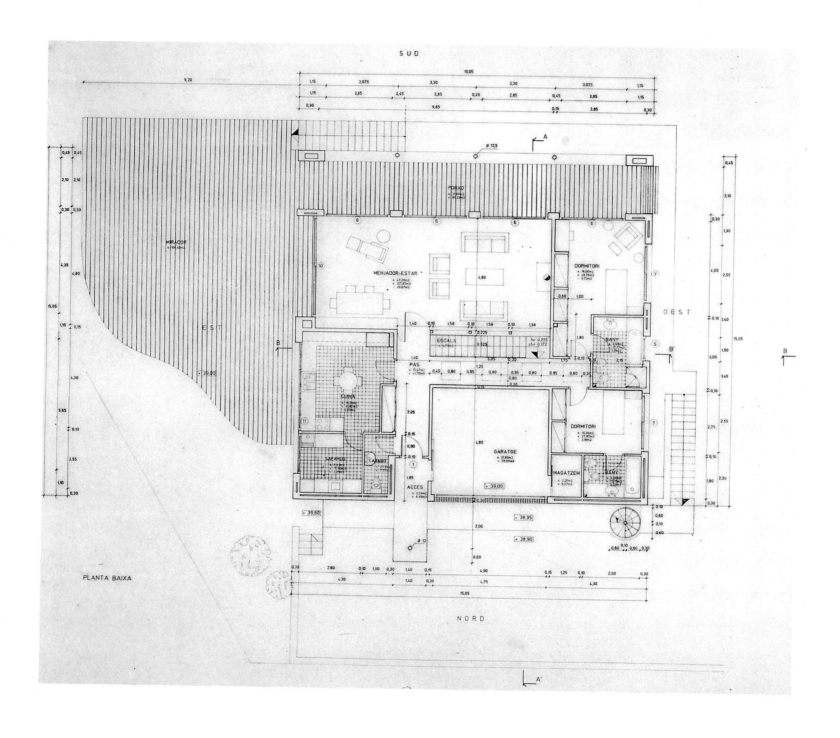

PLANTA BAIXA

140

Sea views to the south

Norman Cinnamond

Single-family dwelling in Aigua Gelida, Girona (Spain) by Norman Cinnamond.

The design for this single-family dwelling by Norman Cinnamond started from the premise of its splendid location. Exposed to the strong sunlight, surrounded by the blue of sea and sky, the golden sands and the bright green vegetation, this mansion towers over the terrain to which it is proud to belong, making its own modest contribution to traditional Mediterranean architecture.

This house is located in Aigua Gelida, in Girona province (Spain), in the most splendid of surroundings: a peninsula stretching out into the Mediterranean, where the residence built right on the seashore commands a spectacular view. One of the site's topographical features, the sharp slope of its terrain, was the determining factor in

the basic arrangement and structure of this building surrounded by a pine forest, a typical feature of the island.

Norman Cinnamond was born in Barcelona in 1941, and studied architecture there, graduating in 1968. Since then he has lectured in projects for more than twenty years at the Escuela Técnica Superior de Arquitectura in Barcelona (1969-1990), and has been visiting lecturer on postgraduate courses at universities in other countries. Among these are the Washington University at Saint Louis (Missouri, 1982) and Harvard University in Cambridge. He was a member of the INFAD board between 1977 and 1979, a member of the ADI-FAD board from 1979 to 1987, a member of the Catalan Autonomous Government's Design Commitee from 1981 to 1982, and he is currently a member of two Catalan

Plan of the main floor.

The pure form of the facade is broken by the black-painted metal helicoidal exterior stairway.

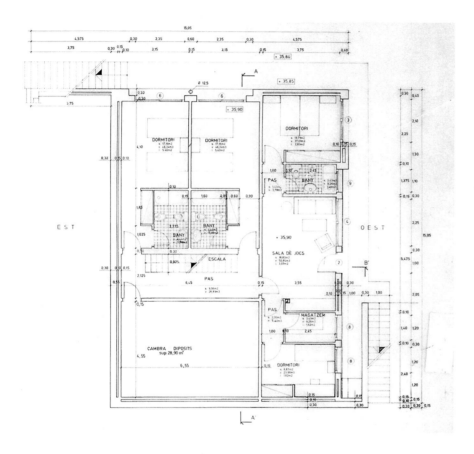

organisations, the Syndicate of Interior Decorators and the Interior Decorators' Cooperative. Norman Cinnamond has been a finalist on several occasions in the prestigious FAD architecture competitions, among others. He has taken part in many such competitions – for example, the planning and design of Torreblanca Park (1984), restoration work on the Records Office in Barcelona (1987) and the design of a Barcelona apartment block (1988). His work has been published in many specialist magazines. He is currently involved in work on six constructions: three residential complexes, an apartment block, the Barcelona Olympic Committee Headquarters and the Muelle del Reloj construction in Barcelona port.

Local regulations dictated that the house be built on two completely separate storeys. The basic idea was that

of a symmetrical design within a square, and the result is a construction in the shape of a 15 x 15 m cube. Access to the dwelling is via the upper floor, through a door which leads into the hall. On the left are a toilet and the kitchen, which contains a table used for snacks and simple meals. At the end of the corridor there is a spacious living room which takes up most of the south elevation. The west wing contains two single bedrooms with en suite bathrooms. On this floor there is also a garage which can accommodate several cars. A staircase in the corridor leads down to the lower floor or basement, which is much smaller and contains three bedroom suites, each with separate bathroom and dressing room, which open out onto the south side, a small flat for the porters, a recreation room leading straight out to the west

Facade facing the street, with the roof of the entrance porch and stairway adding modern touches.

The columns of the exterior veranda with wooden flooring seems to frame the surrounding land and seascape.

Modernity is one of the defining elements of the overall apperance of this single-family dwelling.

The very tall dark green cypress adds a note of verticality to the structure.

View of the entrance showing the exterior stairway and the marine landscape in the distance.

An exterior stone stairway on one corner of the house links the facades.

Opaque glass filters the interior light.

The walls are whitewashed plaster, and the exterior trim is black anodised aluminium.

View of the south facade and the rectangular pool surrounded by wood treated with copper.

facade and also a service area. The entire south facade is protected by a covered veranda which ends in a lookout point facing east. An exterior staricase at one corner of the building gives access to the roof. The outside swimming pool was built between the two floors.

It was essential that the expression of the building be completely planimetric – Normand Cinnamond saw his challenge in the calligraphic definition of the facade design. Maximum exposure to view was a must, and for this reason the only facade where this is not a factor is the rear of the house, facing north towards the road and therefore devoid of any aesthetic interest. The garage and main entrance to the house were built on this side for the same reason. On the other hand, the remaining facades contain large openings facilitating breathtaking views of

the coastline and the Mediterranean. These doors and windows, which are the main device connecting interior and exterior could, however, produce excess heat, especially during the summer months. This potential problem was solved by a system of blinds and shutters which reduces the intensity of the hot sun. In addition, the porch, consisting of a small roof protecting the main entrance, a series of skylights, and the shade provided by the surrounding pine trees also help to control the strong sunlight. It is unusual that the veranda is set into the main cubic unit which forms the dwelling, in such a way that the rectangular openings appear to frame the surroundings as though they were landscape paintings.

Another of the features defining the overall appearance of this single-family dwelling is its modernity.

The wall of the staircase is painted ultramarine grey. View of the first floor passageway.

The large living room/dining room occupies almost the entire southern facade.

The interior flooring is parquet, and the walls are painted white.

The cubic structure is a clear, pure shape which finds contrast in a spiral staircase fixed to one of its exterior corners in an apparent attempt to shatter the geometric forms, its black finish contrasting with the white of the walls. A dark green cypress tree, whose height lends exterior verticality to the construction, also projects above the roof. Mention must also be made of the simple black columns supporting the roof of the veranda and the porch over the main entrance. This is, in a word, an extremely orderly, compact and modern dwelling.

The materials employed in this construction were simple: the whitewashed walls are occasionally combined with stone; all the door and window frames, the columns, the garage door and the exterior staircase were executed in black anodised aluminium. The swimming pool is surrounded by wood treated with copper.

Inside the building the floors are grey and parquet and the walls have been painted white, with the exception of the ultramarine grey staircase wall. Here the woodwork of the door and window frames has been painted white. In the bathrooms, beige synthetic marble has been used alongside white toilet fixtures. The kitchen was faced with grey granite, and once again white was chosen for tiles.

Norman Cinnamond took advantage of this privileged site to build a single-family dwelling characterised by its modern lines, orderliness and compact appearance. The house stretches out towards the surrounding landscape to the south in an attempt to melt into it, and thus provides the opportunity to enjoy each and every one of the fantastic views of the sea.

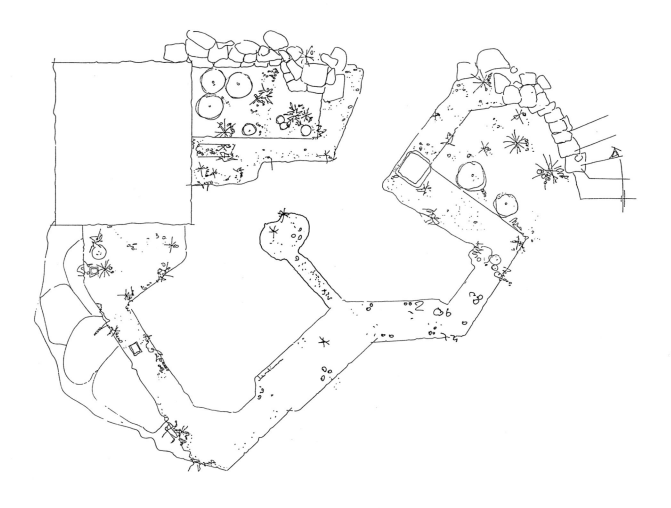

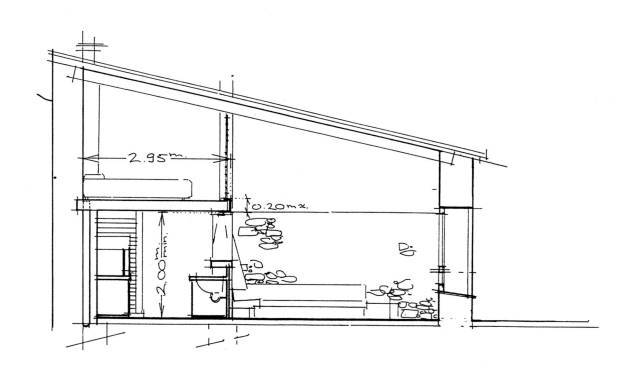

150

Site plan including tower.

Section of one of the rooms of the house.

Architecture and nature

Javier Barba

House by Javier Barba in Menorca.

Once again, Javier Barba has achieved perfect synthesis between the construction itself and the surrounding landscape. Situated in the north of the island of Menorca, itself the most northerly of the Balearic archipelago, this house faithfully conforms to the architectural philosophy of its creator, achieving, in a site bordered by the sea itself, total integration with nature.

Born in Barcelona in 1948, Javier Barba is a founding member of Barba, Bice and Matthews, Architects, based in California, a director and member of Estudio B.C. Architects in Barcelona and a habitual collaborator of L35, Architects. His professional work includes various groups of apartment blocks and single-family dwellings in numerous locations in Catalonia and America, but his

success stems above all from various half-buried or "underground" dwellings which coincide entirely with his concept of ideal architectural design. All this has led to his inclusion in specialised magazines and prestigious newspapers, both national and international. He has also spoken at various conferences in Spain and the United States on the subject of architecture.

The architect's primary aim when he designed this residence was "the construction should be as fully integrated as possible into its immediate surroundings." For Javier Barba, blending the architecture into the landscape is a necessity, and despite the cold currents of new design he maintains that "architecture does not exist as a fashion, rather it is classified as good or bad." His intention when he carried out this project was that the

151

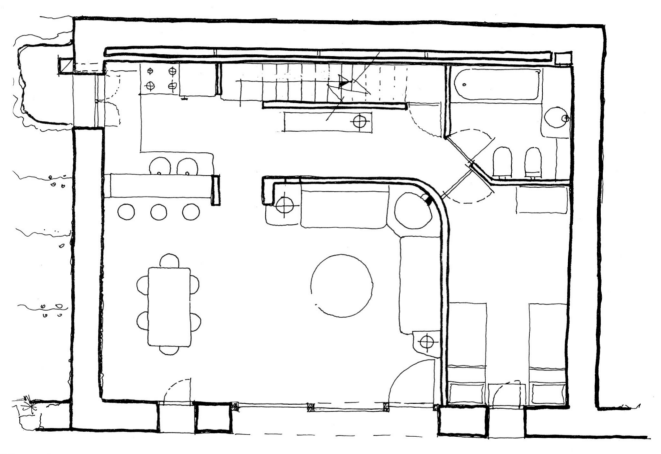

Floor plan of the guest house.

Seen from the sea, the building is practically indistinguishable from its rocky surroundings.

house should fit into the site as if it had always been part of the landscape. This implies positioning each element without creating the slightest disharmony; the structure should be seen as the natural extension of the surroundings, and not as an intrusive element. The culmination of this intention is achieved by the introduction of nature into the actual construction, so that it forms part of it in a natural way. Thus, on the one hand, indigenous plants were planted around and on top of the house, on the terrace, so that the green vegetation would cover the stone walls in the same way as it clothes the mountainside. On the other hand, the large irregularly shaped swimming pool was set in between the rocks so that it is easily confused with the sea.

In order to achieve this harmony, it is also important for the architect to immerse himself in the environment and become imbued with the emotions which it arouses. Therefore Javier Barba considers it vital to visit the site, walk around the area, and even if possible, live there to know it in the sunlight, with the moon, with wind and rain, to learn from which vantage points the views of the landscape are best. All of this enhances the result of the project, and not only solves the problem of imagination but also makes it possible for the architectural work to awaken emotions. Faithful to this ideology, Barba lived on the site for ten days with his family in an old garage, in the singular and idylic framework of the Menorcan coastline, in direct contact with the environment. The plans which produced this dwelling were therefore, conceived

153

Facade of the house with large windows
which open the living room to the exterior.

The house is clad with stone taken from the
excavation on the site itself.

The project was born *in situ* resulting in this house which is respectful of the surrounding natural setting and integrated perfectly into it.

in situ *and implicitly incorporate the message of the architect Frank Lloyd Wright's faithful respect for nature and integration of the construction into its environment.*

One of the constraints on the structuring of this building was the existence of an old fortified tower and the need to adapt the new structure to it. The starting point of the whole design was the most favourable orientation of the house taking into account the general requirements, the preexisting environment's natural light, views of the landscape etc., and blending.

The plans took into account the preexisting construction integrating it into the functional structure of the residence. The original construction was built of sandstone, which was unlike the type of stone excavated from the site and used in the construction of the house. In spite of the

difference, Javier Barba considered it better to use the rock taken from the excavation to face the structure of the new building. This means that the architectural complex forms part of the natural surroundings and comes from them, given that many of the materials used are from this part of the island.

The floor plan of the containing structure, which has an irregular shape, starts from the tower where the entry door and the hall of the residence are situated. From this point the rooms are laid out according to their optimum orientation. Thus, the house has two living rooms, one which opens out onto the terrace, more suitable for the hot season, and another set further into the mountain, where one of the walls is formed from the rock of Monte Toro itself, which is an ideal retreat in winter.

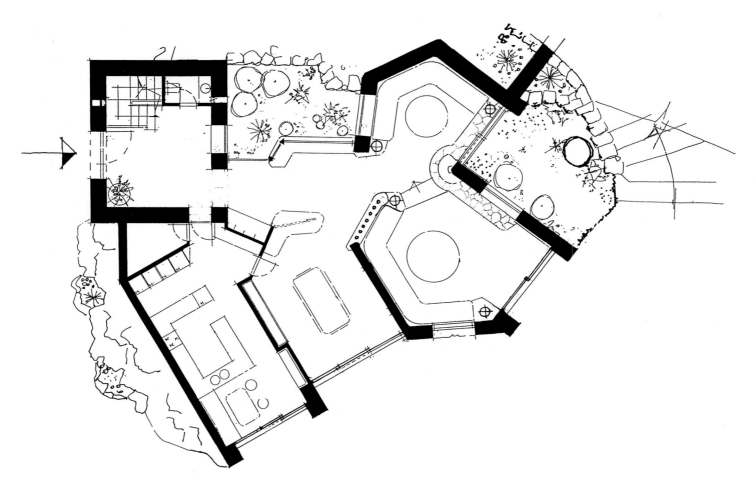

General floor plan, including the tower.

Detail of a porch showing supporting columns made of local bulding materials.

The large, irregularly shaped swimming pool is set in among the rocks.

The idea of integrating the building fully into its setting is also reflected in the interior, both in the materials used, in the methods of construction, and the adequate distribution of natural light, which penetrates the house through strategically placed openings. The fireplace and the benches which appear in various rooms, are typical of Balearic architecture, as is the predominance of the colour white. The paving of the terrace and the exposed wooden beams add to the naturalness and warmth of the atmosphere.

The old garage, where the plans for the house were conceived, has been converted into a guest suite, independent from the main house. The structure has been covered with the same rock used in the construction of the house and decorated in the same style. It has all the facilities necessary to make it a comfortable and welcoming place.

In connection with this project, carried out with the collaboration of the architect Alfredo Vives, Barba also mentioned the inestimable work of the contractors Villalonga y Pons. He also mentioned the interior design work and the choice of furniture, which was mostly bought from antique dealers. This work was done by the owner of the house.

Seen from the sea, the building practically fuses into its surroundings, Javier Barba has once again achieved a building which is an extension of nature rather than an intrusion. As a result of reflection and the time he spent living on the site, he has been able to fit together the beauty of nature and that created by the hand of man.